FRAGILE

Peter Rouse

Mastering the relationships that can make or break a career, and a firm

Contents

Acknowledgements

My thanks to all the bloggers, article writers, essayists, and authors who have fed my imagination over the years, sharing their views on the development of legal services and the profession in a time of accelerated change. The sharing of ideas so freely through business social media is a technology development that I appreciate very much. There is always good content to be found that challenges my preconceptions and opens my mind to new ways of seeing things.

Finally, heartfelt thanks to Rob Edwards, who has been such a stalwart friend—someone with whom I can discuss any subject and be certain of his unfailing intelligence, sensitivity, wisdom, and wicked sense of humour.

Introduction

It is not easy to find happiness in ourselves,
and it is not possible to find it elsewhere.
—Agnes Repplier

I have found that writing a book turns out to be like
anything else you choose to begin: you just have to take the
first step and the rest follows, and later you can tell the story
of why you started and how it turned out. It is with these
words that I began the first edition of this book completed
in late 2005, almost exactly 10 years ago. A second edition
was suggested more than two years ago; however, it has
not felt right until now for me to begin again, integrating
current references into the original work and reflecting my
current perspectives.

So much has emerged and been integrated into
daily life in the past 10 years, predominantly in the field
of information and communications technology, with
consequential impacts in other fields—all of which touch
on our experience, perceptions, beliefs, and the relationship
to our world and each other. When I was writing the first

edition of this book, Facebook had only reached a few US universities, the first iPhone was 18 months away, and "artificial intelligence" (AI) was not being experienced widely as it is today.

As I write this, Search 2.0 and AI-based personal assistants are in the news and in our lives through pervasive apps that demand our attention and resources. IBM, once the behemoth of industry-level computing, is leading again with its AI solution called "Watson," and a number of legal service innovators are reported to be looking into ways in which Watson can be put to work in their arena. Quantum computing is also in the news and "Qubits" may soon be powering AI, accelerating us towards a time when many of the functions and roles we fulfil now will have become redundant. These changes, and the adaptations necessary to integrate them, will challenge lawyers and other legal service providers who serve the needs of individuals and businesses. I see great opportunity for those who are willing to change and great disappointment for those who are not. For now, I admit to being encouraged by the fact that IBM did not name their computer "Holmes."

When drafting the first edition of this book, I made use of voice recognition and vividly recall being so excited at seeing my words appear on screen that I had to look away in order to not be distracted. It worked well enough, saving me a good deal of time and effort as my typing speed was not, and still is not, great. At that time, I had to wear a headset that was plugged into my desktop computer and use a speech recognition application that I had to buy and install. Now I am using the inbuilt microphone in my laptop that has voice recognition as an integral part of its operating system.

Had I written the first edition in 1995, I would likely have dictated it into a portable handset for typing by a secretary. That role of secretary as machine operator translating my thoughts onto the page has been replaced by a low- or no-cost learning technology. Secretaries today are more often personal assistants, usually supporting a number of people, and the many organizational tasks they perform today are again being replaced by apps. What I see happening is a gradual move up the relationship value chain so that more resources can be devoted to the higher functions of relationship. An app such as x.ai may be able to arrange a meeting; it still takes a human, and the pursuit of relationship, to persuade someone to attend.

Information asymmetry is disappearing, and consumers (or "clients," as lawyers think of them) are more demanding than ever. The manner in which client relationships are initiated and conducted has changed significantly due to the accessibility of online resources and social media. Legal practice business models have been fundamentally influenced by the UK's Legal Services Act, whose impact is being felt far beyond its shores. Legal services are being bundled and unbundled; out-sourced and in-sourced; and opened up to competition and innovation as never before. Lawyers are having to revise their ideas about themselves and their place in the services ecosystem.

The IBM Watson website explains its technology as having "a common cognitive framework that humans use to inform their decisions: Observe, Interpret, Evaluate, and Decide." This sounds very similar to what lawyers are expected to do when considering facts and the application of the law. However, there is more to it than that because we humans are also driven by forces less readily defined or contained, and so long as we are the ones making decisions about what is ours, surely we will continue to seek out those who can discern, comprehend, and engage with us fully as human beings. Just as computer technologies are evolving, we as professionals must evolve if we are to serve.

I must admit to being fascinated by technology and how what was science-fiction is becoming social fact so rapidly: haptic technology (e.g., 3D touch), 3D printing, augmented reality, the Internet of Things, data visualization, blockchain technology, and so on. These allow us to interact with people, organizations, and things in new ways, yet we are not evolving at anything like the same pace. That we can broadcast our thoughts to the world by selecting "post" or "send" may enable self-expression. However, it does not mean that we have anything of value to say; in fact, there is so much "noise" generated that we have greater need than ever for information filters—as well as self-restraint.

The ability to jump from flower to flower, screen to screen, app to app, is taking its toll on our capacity for concentration and cognition. Investor pitches are reduced to minutes and preferably a single sentence. Information is shared in 140 characters or less; messages and images can be sent that, once read, self-destruct; language is adapting to convey ideas and feeling states in ever-fewer keystrokes and more elaborate emoticons. Whatever comes, we adapt or sink beneath the waves of passive confusion. Daniel Kahneman's 2011 book, *Thinking, Fast and Slow*, explains our innate tendencies and the role of slow thinking, for which we must make space in our attention or risk missing the prize. The Slow Food movement teaches the benefits of savouring the preparation, consumption, and sharing of food;

so too we can see how we miss out when we don't give time to sharing, exploring, and shaping ideas and ourselves through real conversation with others. Reality, as a subjective and a community experience, is best augmented by giving complete attention.

My career in law started in 1977 when I attended the Part 1 course at the College of Law in Guildford, UK. I spent some time working for a three-- partner firm in Henley-on-Thames, eventually finding a traineeship ("Articles of Clerkship," as they were known then) with a slightly larger firm in Reading that began in September 1979. After a year away for the final examination, I had the good fortune to transfer the last six months of my traineeship to Lovell White & King in 1983 (now "Hogan Lovells"). Then on to Barlow Lyde & Gilbert; then back to Lovells before moving out to Asia in 1987 with Baker & McKenzie. In 1990, I returned to the UK and set up my own firm, an organization that I led for 10 years and that is still known as "Rouse."

As to my credentials for writing this book, they are founded primarily in my years in the profession and from a vivid recollection of the various stages of growing up from paralegal to trainee, to associate, to partner, to senior partner and leader, to consultant and commentator. I have, since 2000, had the great privilege of time for learning and reflection, for discovering so much that I wish I had known then, finding meaning and purpose now so many other ways, including writing about and sharing what I know now. If enough people tell you to write about it, and if the inner compulsion is strong enough, then in the end resistance is useless.

Committing ideas or information to writing is an exacting process. It tests you. It demands of you that you set down what can never be undone once published. This is something lawyers have to live with day in and day out, and I well remember being told by the eminent speaker at the Law Society ceremony for the newly qualified to "write every letter as though a judge might read it out in open court." What we can only ever strive to do is our best: to give it our full attention and then let it go out. In constructing this second edition, I have read and evaluated every line to be sure that it is what I find to be true for me at this time.

What I set out to do with the first edition and do again now is to record ideas and practices that I have discovered for myself and that others have given to me to pass on; not all, just what come together naturally and seem most important at this time. I don't know anymore where some came from, where the line is between what I have learned and what came from me. There is, of course, nothing new under the sun, and I am at best an interpreter. If you recognize ideas in these pages, then I will be delighted if my way of expressing them makes sense.

I have written about what I know from my own experience and believe to be valuable. The practices I recommend I am practicing, though not always. I struggle to listen to people as I should and not to interrupt; I wrestle with things when I should trust my self and the process, simply forming a clear intention and allowing it to happen; I still eat and drink what is not good for my body from time to time. I am traveling; I have not arrived.

The pursuit of authenticity is a deserving preoccupation; find it and the rest, including the occupation that is right for you, will follow. Whatever your reasons for becoming a legal professional, there are so many good reasons for staying on and for finding a real life in legal practice. Law is a reified system of values whereas its practice is a vocation, or can be. Vocation requires participation; you have to be fully engaged and through it express and explore yourself and your own authenticity. You have to be the author of your own authentic practice. None of this is easy; as Yogi Berra put it: "In theory, there is no difference between theory and practice. In practice, there is."

Legal education may have changed, but when I did mine it was all about how much you could remember. The real stuff has to be learned at the coal face with colleagues and clients and from people who learned in the same way. It is very hard not to imprint on authority figures, not to mimic language, behaviour, and even mannerisms. Others lead by example, and we learn by that example. I witnessed some pretty strange and aggressive behaviour while in my traineeship and later in my career. I saw a great deal that I was determined to escape and never to emulate, and later learned to understand how I often failed in that intent.

It seems to me that while we are taught about the law, we are not taught anything of the life skills needed to manage ourselves, our relationships with colleagues and clients, and our "private lives" in the hugely demanding conditions of legal practice. The fact that lawyers are well paid is no answer; that is simply a matter of supply and demand. If you consider your "compensation" to be compensating you for the harm you suffer, then you need to do something about it. There is no reason why lawyers cannot make good money doing what they love. However, you do have to love it or no amount of money will compensate you for a life squandered. If you value your time here, then invest yourself in making the most of the experience.

What you find in this book can only become useful if you bring whatever grabs you into your own experience, if you really try it out and see what happens. This might be called a self-help book, though not of the "grow your own denim, knit your own yogurt" variety. This is a book about what people refer to as the "soft stuff," and yet it is the really hard stuff. It is about self-management, cognition, and excellence. You will be challenged to the extent of your willingness to look at yourself, your relationships, your practice, your behaviour, and your organization differently.

You will, I hope, find questions and ideas that cause you to question. You will not find lists of suggestions and practical tips; there are already books that do this very well. While I have highlighted some particular forms of behaviour that I know to be conducive to building and sustaining trust in working relationships, I believe that it is up to you to find your way of expressing yourself, your values, and your organization. Other people's ideas can get you started, give you confidence, and even ignite your own creativity. I have lots of ideas, but what is best for you will come from you if you let it; what is best for your organization will come from everyone if you let it.

The threads that run through this book are to do with the "inner game": the richness and reward of becoming fully involved in what is going on inside you and at the same time building the capacity to see differently what is going on around you and your part in creating it—you as co-author of your relationships with colleagues and clients. What I believe is that we need an "inside out" perspective on the world about us that recognizes the influence that our "inner view" has on our experience, rather than an "outside in" view that treats life and experience as something that is done to us. Life passes through our experiential filters and it is our challenge, if we choose to accept it, to know and refine those filters.

Rather than writing about legal services as a business, my focus is on learning about effectiveness in relationships on behalf of your business, for yourself and for the organization. This is the new field of advantage and one that offers longer-lasting success in business and quality in life. I believe that the capacities and life skills I am addressing are what are needed to make the practice of law sustainable and profitable. Given the rapid development of AI and its ability to handle work that would once have been done by secretaries, paralegals, and, before long, lawyers, surely it makes sense to focus on what sets us apart from computer intelligence.

1

Relationships

Professional life presents tremendous challenges. It challenges
us not just in the context of the skills and intelligence we are
expected to apply but, more importantly, in the context of
the relationships that arise in the course of our daily work.
These relationships determine our sense of self-worth, our
well-being, and the success of the business in which we
operate.

If we're not careful, we can quite literally lose ourselves
in our work. For our own protection and for the purposes
of assimilation into our immediate professional context,
we can too easily adopt behaviours so divorced from our
private selves and so alien to our core values that we become
disconnected and, ultimately, dysfunctional.

Whatever our activity, whatever the nature of the skills
we bring to bear, we are as professionals engaged in service.
To be engaged in service is, at its highest, to participate in
a process that recognizes the truth of our interdependence
and realizes the power of our interconnection. At its worst,
service becomes a source of anxiety, insecurity, blame, and
recrimination.

BUSINESS IMPERATIVES

Let me be clear from the outset that business performance is of central importance to all that you will find in these pages. Business provides the context, the means, and the profit and is inextricably entwined with practice performance. No one wants a great firm with a poor business and none could sustain it—if the practice doesn't pay, the people won't stay. The business is both a servant and a master in a legal practice.

Key dynamics to consider that have a direct bearing on business performance and profitability, and are directly impacted by human factors and relationships, are:

Cost of Conversion

This concerns the cost of chargeable hours recorded and the conversion ratios between those hours recorded and the hours billed and fees collected; for example, for every 100 hours recorded, 90 hours are billed and 85 hours are collected. Ultimately, what matters is the amount of hours collected. Ideally, of course, the ratio is 1:1:1; every hour recorded is billed and collected.

The number of hours recorded is a simple measure of utilization: how many hours each fee earner records. The cost of those hours includes the salary or drawings of the fee earner, the support staff cost, and an apportionment of all other overhead. The more efficiently, and willingly, these resources are applied, the better the ratio between recorded and billed hours becomes. The relationships in play here are largely internal to the firm. The business challenge lies in the best use and direction of the resources of the firm, which comprise first and foremost human resources.

The rate of conversion to hours collected is determined by a number of factors all concerned with management of client relationships, including ability to pay. Fixed-fee billing requires even greater discipline and understanding of utilization, as the cost of time spent by fee earners is invariably the highest overhead the business has to carry. Collected fees are the oxygen of the business.

Cost of Sales

This is the cost of acquiring, developing, and retaining clients; all the marketing costs and non-chargeable time invested in building brand, profile, market presence, and generally winning business. Acquiring new clients is always a priority for any firm because this is one path to revenue growth. Development is the extension of the client relationship into one that produces repeat work and new areas of work. Retention is about maintaining, deepening, and refreshing the client relationship in order to remain relevant to the client and the client's business or personal needs.

All this is the stuff of presentation, personality, and service relationships.

Cost of Recruitment

This cost includes the cost of attracting talent to the firm, the cost of training, and the cost of retention. Partner and staff loyalty and retention should be of major concern to any firm because replacement costs are high in every sense: constant changes are unsettling and often disruptive, however well they may be handled.

Reducing costs has a direct impact on profitability so long as doing so is sustainable and does not undermine the fabric and assets of the firm. Greater profitability translates into greater scope for distribution of profits to owners and staff and for investment in training, technology, and growth.

EVERY RELATIONSHIP MATTERS

In the world of professional service, relationships are of central importance. Professional relationships should not be regarded as simply transactional assets to be acquired, adjusted, or discarded; they have the potential to be meaningful, lasting, and profoundly rewarding. The journey to such relationships begins with open and sincere dialogue and progresses according to the age-old principle that you get out what you put in. Though there may be superficial distinctions between them, relationships with colleagues and relationships with clients can and should be given the same attention and respect.

The key components of a client–lawyer relationship can be broken down to four simple areas: functional, financial, intellectual, and emotional. Among law firms of a certain scale—whether small, medium, or large—peer firms within the same tier are likely to be indistinguishable in terms of their functional, financial, and intellectual components. This leaves one key differentiator that can deliver success and future growth—namely, personality. The quality of individual human interactions and relationships within and outside a firm establishes its personality and "style." This is what lies at heart of the "chemistry" that so often lawyers and clients alike refer to when describing relationships that really work.

Lawyers are immersed in a variety of relationships that create their own particular problems, including their relationships to the law itself, to the profession, to colleagues, to superiors, and to clients. These relationships arise from the particular roles that we take on in the practice of the law. They are roles and relationships that deserve particular attention and demand a deliberate awareness in order to ensure they do not distort our relationships with ourselves and with others, causing stress and harm. We have to be mindful of these influences and their cumulative impact on our perceptions and our actions.

Stress arises, for the most part, from anything that represents a threat to ourselves, whether direct or indirect, that has occurred or may occur. The reality of the human condition is that we feel and fear a great deal more threat to our well-being than is actually real. However, perceived threats to our roles and relationships are as real and as physiologically and psychologically disruptive as are threats to our physical security.

Chuck Spezzano, founder of Psychology of Vision, puts it simply in his book, *If It Hurts, It Isn't Love*: "There is no problem that is not at some level a relationship problem." Take a moment to think about any problem you have and consider at what level it may be a problem to you because it involves a relationship between you and another or the relationship you have with yourself.

Knowledge of self is the only real starting point and foundation for relationship with others. The simple reason for this is that others share with us and are separated from us by a common condition—namely, the human condition. Self-knowledge is a condition from which self-management becomes possible. Self-management is an essential platform for authenticity, leadership, and management of others. Relationships with self, with others, with nature, and with things are what define our human experience. If you are someone for whom the best things in life are not things, then I hope to persuade you that "Every Relationship Matters" (ERM) is a valuable guiding principle by which to live and practice law.

TRUST

As technology has taken hold, as the pace of business life has quickened, so have trusted relationships become ever more important. Trust brings with it expectations that must be shared and understood by all concerned. Trust is not a one-sided thing; it can and should be a mutual condition in any relationship.

Between client and professional advisor there must be trust going both ways. If not—if the professional or client harbour distrust at any level—then the relationship will never reach its potential.

Trust is essentially about expectations. When we say that we trust someone, there is attached to that trust a string of expectations, many of which may never be expressed; these include assumptions such as honest intent, mutuality, and priority. The result can be that in giving our trust to someone, we in fact impose upon that person expectations that he or she has not consented to or agreed to meet. In working relationships with others inside and outside our firms, it is all too easy for unexpressed and unmet expectations to lead to disappointment and a sense of being "let down"—or worse, to be considered a breach of trust that brings an end to the relationship.

Establishing trust is about managing expectations: identifying, articulating, and adjusting expectations from day to day as circumstances demand. It is your job as a service provider to elicit from clients their expectations and then to ensure that they are addressed, always in a context of mutuality—one that recognizes your expectations as equal in importance. Where there is a mismatch in expectations, there is a source of conflict and stress.

Our behaviours can promote trust or undermine it. In Chapter 11, I have set out some suggestions as to behaviours that serve to build and reinforce trust. One I will highlight here is that of acknowledgement. If you provide your clients or the market with your e-mail address, then you should expect it to be used and ensure that every e-mail is answered, if only by an automated message saying that the sender can expect a substantive response in, say, 48 hours and perhaps suggesting alternative routes of communication in cases of urgency. Similarly, if you have a Twitter account and accept direct messages on that account, then you should be ready to respond to them.

The world of social media is characterized by acknowledgement and responsiveness. To "like" or "favourite" or "share" is part of the dance that is socializing online. It is an ecosystem driven by reciprocity that is fundamental to our nature; it now literally reinforces the adage that what goes around comes around.

We are constantly monitoring the signals from each other to assess our relationships. Sending the right signals is what it is all about. It is the little things that make the difference: simple demonstrations of respect and consideration that count for so much.

FAIR EXCHANGE

Trust is essential to knowledge sharing and to the creation of community. Energy is invested by the individual and exchanged in communication, innovation, and creativity at every level of complexity. Trust is the condition in which that energy can flow freely.

In *The Conductive Organization*, Hubert Saint-Onge and Charles Armstrong define knowledge as "the capability to take effective action." They distinguish between knowledge access—access to a stock of recorded information— and knowledge exchange—the exchange of knowledge among people and organizations—and they describe the purpose of the knowledge exchange: to "build new capabilities and deepen relationships."

Another manifestation of relationships key to modern business is the idea of community—communities of interest and of practice, clusters, teams, and other short-hand terms for collaborative groups of individuals. Max De Pree, in the preface to his book *Leadership Is an Art*, has this to say about community:

> Community is where it happens. In communities we are all given opportunities and the chance to make the most of them. Only in communities can we set meaningful goals and measure our performance. Only in communities do we grow and prosper as persons and reach our potential. Only in communities do we respect and honor and thank the people who contribute to our interdependent lives.

In legal practice, we are part of a number of interlocking and interrelated communities through which we can discover and refine ourselves. This is rich ground for service to our own aspirations and to others, not in a compartmentalized way, but rather in an integrated way that acknowledges boundaries while honouring interdependence. As Ted Nelson put it so beautifully in *Computer Lib/Dream Machines*, "Everything is deeply intertwingled."

VOLUNTEERS

Looking beyond the legal and financial structure that constitutes a firm, beyond name and numbers, a professional firm is an aggregation of individuals who have agreed to work together in a single organization. Think of how a firm comes into being in the first place. One or more qualified lawyers decide they would like to work together in practice. One day, the first day, they gather together in chosen premises, or simply under a chosen name, and begin that practice. This is a voluntary process and one that is, in effect, repeated each day that the members of the firm, including all staff, voluntarily come together.

The organization Tomorrow's Company pioneers corporate social responsibility, and some years ago developed the proposition of "license to operate." The idea behind this proposition is that every business organization operates only with the consent of a number of groups: shareholders, employees, local community, governing bodies, national government, and society. In much the same way, legal professional firms also operate by the consent of the partners, associates, support staff, suppliers, clients, professional governing body, and so on.

Such consent can be given freely and willingly, or it can be forced and given grudgingly; consent can also be withdrawn. There are many examples of even major professional firms that have collapsed as a result of what has essentially been the withdrawal of consent. Such withdrawal of consent is invariably based in a fundamental lack of confidence; indeed, it is a vote of "no confidence" in which people vote with their feet.

There may have been particular triggers, specific events or challenges, or just financial problems that lit the fire; how many of these fires would have taken hold in these firms had their cultures not already been brittle and tinder dry? How confident are you that your firm would survive should a challenge present itself? How truly loyal are the members of your firm? If you believe them to be loyal, what are they loyal to? Extreme examples, perhaps, and happily few are tested; nevertheless, the questions remain. What keeps your firm together? What drives it to achieve, to survive, and to thrive?

Some are in practice for the money and the power. Research has shown that the accumulation of wealth does little to dampen a desire for more; history shows that the same goes for power. You may have an idea who those people are within your own firm, although you may be wrong about them. Money and power are in the end not enough to keep someone loyal who believes that income and authority are entirely deserved and can be obtained elsewhere, in another firm.

For the most part, firms continue to operate simply because they exist. Individual partners and staff of a firm will have very different ideas as to why they come to work each day. For some it is because they have no other ideas as to what they could do or where they should work (until an alternative presents itself that is as convincing as their present reality, at which point they may forget that though the grass may well look greener, it still tastes of grass).

Many experience unease simply because their values and aspirations are not clearly and consciously placed within the contextual framework of the firm. This unease can lead to alienation and distrust, which in turn undermine participation and performance. Think what could be achieved if it were possible to involve every individual such that each finds expression of their individual meaning and purpose within the embrace of the work and values of the firm. Think of the energy unleashed individually and collectively. Finding meaning and purpose, achieving authenticity in one's own life, is the most profound and rewarding concern any of us engage with. It is a noble cause, an internal compulsion; obstructing it leads to discontent and unease.

In the world of education we have seen a substantial shift in recent years, and certainly since I was at school, towards building confidence and encouraging individual expression. Educators have come to recognize that children and young people give their best in an atmosphere of encouragement, reassurance, and support. They don't just talk about unique talents; they provide a framework within which those talents can safely flourish and find expression. The world of business needs that talent in order to be able to deliver the innovation that can mean the difference between success and failure in the creation of future value.

Rather than placing human energies in harness, business is slowly coming to recognize the need to create the conditions in which those humans can deliver what no organizational system or software solution can. This is particularly recognized in the high-speed and high-growth world of technology startups, where the difference between success and failure comes down to the people involved and how they work together. Collaborative working apps such as Slack and Salesforce have become essential tools for keeping everyone engaged and sharing. Biodiversity is considered vital to the security of our future capacity to feed the world; diversity offers the same promise for humankind in the increasingly complex world we are co-creating. Diversity needs space to do its work, and that space comes from developing cultures within organizations that encourage people to contribute more and be more than adjuncts to machinery.

For many reasons specific to legal professional service, the legal profession still finds it extremely difficult to embrace diversity, change, or uncertainty in any form. The fear of being criticized or rejected by clients, reprimanded or punished by our professional governing body, sued for negligence, or otherwise embarrassed leaves lawyers with their backs to the wall, smiling bravely in the face of public adversity. Most lawyers consider themselves to be, and probably to a large extent are, "between a rock and a hard place."

The accelerating pace of the world today, together with the ever-increasing demands and varied expectations of clients, places immense pressures on legal professionals and their staff. Clients do not see, and so do not understand, what goes on behind the scenes. The general public simply does not grasp just how much is involved in delivering legal service. The legal profession struggles to explore and manage client expectations while living with the constant fear of losing clients to the ever-present competition. Many lawyers are too busy to get help and too busy to help themselves to establish a better balance in their service relationships.

What many legal practices have done is to try to leverage technology to achieve automation of traditional practices rather than seeking transformation. I think it is time to ask fundamental questions about what lawyers and law firms are for. I believe that there is a great deal lawyers have to contribute to society, to business, and to the individual. The opportunity is there to be taken if lawyers can rediscover their essential vocation and have the courage to step out of the traditional approaches to service to create the new norms that so many clients are impatiently seeking.

The Legal Tech sector has seen significant investment in recent years, and those firms, like the so-called challenger banks, are cutting new paths into the legal services market. The pathways that you see in the countryside when walkers have left the usual trail or road to reach their endpoint more directly are known as, I have been told, "lines of desire." Challenger firms are offering the legal service equivalent of such "lines of desire," offering clients shortcuts to meeting their needs. The new paths may be narrow for now, but the more they are used, the more others will notice and use them.

LEADERSHIP

The prevailing view among managers has long been that the most effective management method is KITA: the "kick in the ass." I'm not going to suggest that this method cannot be effective or pretend that I have not used it at times myself. However, it is not dissimilar to consuming a large amount of sugar: it delivers a short-term rush of energy, inevitably followed by a crash. If you keep using sugar, you will have to increase the dose to achieve the same effect, and gradually performance will deteriorate or completely break down.

There are times when we all need to be helped through a crisis of inaction and indecision by a leader or friend who can be direct. However, finding resolve within ourselves is always the surest way to develop our personal strength and power. Encouraging colleagues to find their own power is the mark of a confident manager and leader willing to allow others to grow. Understanding and working with people and their humanity is emotional intelligence.

One view of leadership is that it is a quality and an activity that can and should be exercised at every level within a business as circumstances demand and as the particular qualities and skills of the individual allow. However, what I would like to look at here is the role of leadership from the point of view of those who are "in charge" in a legal practice.

Having made partner, we may be confident, for a while at least, that we have achieved our professional goals through attaining a position of power, ownership, and authority; this is, however, just the beginning. Once achieved, the power afforded by authority can be used in such a way as to return rewards that go beyond financial gain and outlast the pleasures of material advantage.

The opportunity is to engage sincerely in discovering the aspirations of all those under your authority and wherever possible channeling individual energies to the good of the individual and the firm. This opportunity is an opportunity for service—an opportunity to give.

> *"Life is a gift, bearing a gift, which is the art of giving."*
>
> —*Dee Hock, Birth of the Chaordic Age*

Kindness and discipline are not mutually exclusive. The discipline with which lawyers must practice does not preclude opportunity for change, growth, personal development, meaningful relationship, and service. Yet, for many lawyers in practice, it does.

In his book *Synchronicity*, Joseph Jaworski, a US lawyer who created, among other things, the American Leadership Forum, put it this way:

> Leadership is all about the release of human possibilities. One of the central requirements for good leadership is the capacity to inspire the people in the group: to move them and encourage them and pull them into the activity, and to help them get centered and focused and operating at peak capacity. A key element of this capacity to inspire is communicating to people that you believe they matter, that you know they have something important to give. The confidence you have in others will to some degree determine the confidence they have in themselves.

My own experience of the best teachers I have encountered is that I felt from them the confidence that I had it in me to achieve what they asked of me. They also taught me that what I asked of myself was often some way off the mark and more often than not actually hindered my way forward. In me, this invariably surfaces as trying too hard to perform and focusing more on form than on taking my time to find true understanding through practice. I think my teachers and coaches have always recognized and worked with that part of me while encouraging mature dedication to practice so as to allow my abilities to emerge and evolve at their own pace.

I believe I have always had similar confidence, and one might say faith, in those I have worked with in legal practice. There was never greater reward for me as a leader of my own firm than to witness an individual discover his or her abilities, to witness the recognition within themselves of their own power to achieve what they once thought was beyond their reach. After a while, such individuals come to know themselves better and so become better able to provide leadership for themselves and ultimately for others.

In order to lead well you need to love it; you need to be having fun and recognize that that is what everyone else wants too. Dee Hock, founder and CEO emeritus of the Visa organization, speaks in his book *Birth of the Chaordic Age* of leadership as a process through which people are induced to behave in a particular way—rather than compelled to do so. Looked at in this way, leadership is about coaching and coaxing an individual towards flow, towards complex experience and personal growth in the context of the opportunities for such experience presented by the business. This is leadership in its truest sense, in contrast to traditional ideas of management through command and control. Care, guidance, coaching, and support are essential and yet so often lacking in legal practices.

SELF MANAGEMENT

> *"[T]he first and paramount responsibility is to manage one's self; one's own integrity, character, wisdom, knowledge, time, temperament, words and acts. It is a complex, and never ending, incredibly difficult, oft-shunned task, without which no person is fit for authority no matter how much they acquire. Managing self should have at least a third of our time, ability and energy."*
>
> *—Dee Hock, Birth of the Chaordic Age*

To make our way through each day causing the least harm to others and to ourselves requires concentration—presence of mind and body. Perhaps twenty times a day we will need to check and rebalance ourselves to be sure that we are not carrying internal struggles over issues past and future into our interactions with others. We need to notice first when we are not here, in this moment, but elsewhere. We then need to bring ourselves into this moment in order to be able to release our intelligence, our intuition and insight, from the entanglement of preoccupation with our thoughts about ourselves.

When we are free of preoccupation, we have the capacity to see those we are asked to manage and the wider context in which that management role has a place. Though we may be engaged in managing risk, we are mistaken if we believe that those over whom we have authority are not capable of recognizing such risk and acting appropriately to minimize or mitigate that risk. To think that way is to undermine those who of necessity we must trust to get the job done and, in addition, to undermine ourselves as the ones who chose to recruit them. Dee Hock, in *Birth of the Chaordic Age*, again:

> Management inevitably has to do with hiring, motivating, directing, and correcting those over whom one has authority. That perception has some utility in a world of mechanistic, industrial age organizations in which the creation and control of constants, uniformity and efficiency is paramount, but that world is evaporating in front of our eyes and the old perception is increasingly useless in a world where the need has become the understanding and coordination of variability, complexity and effectiveness.

The metaphor that comes to my mind when thinking about management relates to my experience of classical horsemanship and dressage. In this discipline, there is a practice called "half halt," which involves a subtle closing of the hand, a momentary hold and release of the rein contact. The purpose is to ask the horse to rebalance, to collect itself, in order to make a smooth transition into another direction or pace. The rider maintains a gentle contact throughout so that the horse is guided yet free to move as directed. Clear signals, encouragement, and reassurance are the way to induce flowing movement and the precision such movement makes possible.

Though you may have no experience of horsemanship, I am sure you understand the point. In the case of a horse, you are dealing with perhaps 3,500 pounds of animal capable of causing harm to itself and to you; in the case of a human being, you are dealing with something very similar, only smaller. The fight-or-flight response is one that is being constantly activated in every one of us, causing what is known as "cortical inhibition" (a fancy way of saying "can't think straight"). This physiological response releases hormones within the body that allow immense short-term releases of energy, yet they cause long-term damage to our health and life expectancy when they continue unabated. Creating a supportive environment is essentially about creating an environment in which that fight-or-flight response is activated as little as possible by leaders, managers, and colleagues.

I am convinced that self-management should be a priority for every one of us, beginning with practice leaders, who may then in turn ask the same of those they lead. The benefits of self-management include the capacity to promote positive emotion, to find personal growth and satisfaction, and to establish meaning and purpose. Far from being a chore, this is a process of self-discovery that brings huge challenges and commensurate rewards.

SOFT STUFF, HARD STUFF

The importance of personal development and values to business life is increasingly being recognized and accepted even among lawyers; take, for example, the excellent contributions from Jeena Cho in the *Above the Law* online magazine. People in all walks of business life are at one stage or another likely to encounter some form of training, mentoring, coaching, or counselling in the course of their careers. Personal and organizational transformation are becoming mainstream disciplines rather than being seen as "alternative" indulgences. I believe them to be the key to a successful business and lasting professional relationships and, therefore, to sustainable business and profitability. The so-called soft side of business is being actively deployed as a source of personal and commercial advantage. In truth, it is anything but soft; it may be the hardest stuff you have ever dealt with.

The law is an exacting profession, and to maintain a leading position requires the highest standards and quality of service. Lawyers and staff are expected to perform in spite of the pressures that exist in this competitive and demanding service industry. In addition, partners carry responsibility for practice leadership, management, and development. Legal practice is not for the fainthearted; the intellectual and relationship demands are rigorous and there is no margin for error.

There are limits to what good risk management systems and information technology can do. The rest is down to human factors: intellectual acuity, relationship building, trust, discipline, and energy. These human factors deliver the personality, flexibility, creativity, and resilience that underpin sustainable service success. There is only so much that management can do to elicit maximum performance, only so many incentives that can be used to encourage focus and application.

Critical issues directly affecting financial performance and growth include sickness/absence, "presenteeism," partner and associate loyalty, and client retention and development. At the heart of these is the tough stuff of human perception, behaviour, and relationships.

> *"There is persuasive evidence that there is a clear relation between positive emotion at work, high productivity, low (staff) turnover, and high loyalty."*
> —*Martin E. P. Seligman, PhD, Authentic Happiness*

My purpose in this book is to explore key issues in professional life that are grounded in the hard practicalities of day-to-day practice. In doing so, I draw on my own experience of legal professional and business life and what I have learned from others along the way. It is not my aim, nor my place, to lay out a prescription for success or the proper conduct of a professional individual or business. I simply wish to draw attention to various factors that influence our personal and business experience, put forward for consideration what makes up the intensely human experience that is professional life, and make some practical suggestions that I believe readers will find useful and profitable.

Summary

- Relationships are of central importance to professional services and thrive in conditions of trust

- Building and maintaining trust is all about managing expectations and underpinned by a thorough understanding of what others expect

- Trust promotes knowledge sharing and active cooperation within organisations and other communities of interest

- Everyone in an organisation is a volunteer and working relationships operate by consent which can be withheld, to one degree or another, or withdrawn

- Productive collaboration and innovation is achieved by creating the conditions in which volunteers can best release and direct their energies

- Leadership that coaches individuals towards their potential is replacing 'command and control' and KITA management styles in many sectors

- Self-management is an essential skill for leaders and vital to constructive leadership in modern business

- Self-management supports positive emotion; achieving personal growth and satisfaction; and finding meaning and purpose

- Until you can exercise, if not master, self-management you cannot ask it of others

- Addressing the human factors that so profoundly impact performance is challenging and yet essential for all seeking sustained growth and profitability

The Impact of Artificial Intelligence

While it may be stimulating, even exhilarating, to explore possible futures in which machines seek to dominate man, or in which computers become integrated with humans so as to influence human behaviour, such scenarios are at best a distraction from the more likely and immediate impact of artificial intelligence (AI). This fear of being overtaken by technology is already beginning to spread among the legal community, promoted by those who know that readers avidly consume such stories.

The term IT is now commonplace and refers to everything in the field of information and communication technologies. In order to characterize and position the role of AI, I find it helpful to think of assistive technology, which I will abbreviate to AT. The role of AT is to anticipate and act based on predictable and actual user choices. Rather than requiring the user to make multiple sequential choices and actions, AT acts to reduce or eliminate the need for predictable actions to be undertaken by the user. AT is an application of AI as it is today—namely, a rule-based tool that has to be taught how to function. AI that is capable of sophisticated, independent, unsupervised learning is being explored; however, it is likely some way off. If I ever write a third edition of this book, ten years from now, then this form of AI may well have become a reality; what is more likely is that humankind will not have changed.

Examples of what I am calling AT are merging into mainstream life as I write, including Microsoft's Cortana, Google Now, "M" from Facebook, and Apple's Siri. There are now so many apps in play that deploying the ones you want to use is itself consuming a great deal of time and personal energy, and the response to this is the creation of "invisible" apps that use sensors and other data to offer more complex and complete options for users that can then be actioned. This incremental innovation is moving at a tremendous pace, fueled by latent demand from hard-pressed users, extraordinary reach and capacity for adoption via mobile technology, and the combination of human ingenuity with venture funding.

In contrast with what may have been the case in the past, the integration of computer technology into our daily lives is being driven by personal rather than business demand. We have become avid consumers of intelligent devices that, like many time-saving devices, require a good deal of time to purchase, learn, operate, and maintain. We are becoming ever more adept at assimilating these devices into our daily lives and a degree of dependency is unquestionably developing, such that many of us cannot imagine being parted from them or imagine how we would manage without them. Connecting these devices into an "Internet of Things" is underway, along with an increasingly important role for voice recognition as the primary means of interaction with the user.

I remember reading an article many years ago about how Mercedes was investing in research that would make driving safer by removing as many decisions as possible from the driver. This notion has always amused me as it points to what we must accept to be true about ourselves—namely, our all-too-easily degraded attention and responses. A driverless car is anathema to a car enthusiast. The arrival of legal project management is an uncomfortable prospect for lawyers who have always managed litigation by "feel" rather than process design and management. Anti-lock braking systems have unquestionably had a huge impact on safety and at the same time made it possible to drive faster. Clever uses of various technologies in legal services undoubtedly serve to reduce mistakes and increase speed while also bringing down costs.

Machines perform repetitive mechanical tasks better than humans do, and whenever businesses can remove humans from roles that make them merely adjuncts to machines, they do. This holds true for robotics in use in car plants and for tasks such as data analysis and visualization. There are legal tech and service businesses encroaching on the territory formally occupied by lawyers and legal support staff. At the same time, US labour statistics show that paralegal jobs are expected to grow significantly, which suggests that who does what work is also changing.

There are ever more tools being made available online so that clients can help themselves and be better routed to the specialist legal support they really need. Some law firms have made precedent documents freely available on their sites because they recognize that this is not only what many clients want, but it also serves to pre-qualify clients who really need their services so they better understand the value they obtain by paying for expert help and guidance. I have had firsthand experience of an induction process for new clients operated by a firm to which a legal expenses insurer referred me. I dealt with someone who worked to a specific script and whose job it was to obtain from me information that would allow me to proceed to the next stage of the process. This could have been done online; however, I could see how it would work well for many clients. After all, I don't expect to be checked in for a flight by the captain of the aircraft.

We can expect to see what might be described as a streamlining of the legal service vehicles in which clients choose to travel and, with it, genuine improvements in their service experiences. Expectations as to what a service experience should be like will be led by other services that genuinely strive to please and keep you coming back for more. Much of what we call loyalty is dependent on a person's need for what you offer and your ability to serve that need in a manner and at a cost that are acceptable. You may "acquire" a client, but never confuse their choice with any entitlement to their work. You have an opportunity to serve and no more.

SENTIMENT

Discussion of AI, including what I have called AT, is useful as a means of identifying those facets of the human experience, and consequently those parts of the legal service experience, to which AI is not suited and may never be. The area in which we often struggle to understand others and ourselves is that of emotions or feelings. As legal service professionals, we may see our role as one of providing objective and rational analysis and guidance working within the framework of the law. It may seem outlandish to suggest it, but perhaps our more important and more-needed role is as story tellers and interpreters of dreams.

Nonsense, you say. Allow me to explain.

To begin with, it may be reassuring to know that computers are very good with data but very poor at discerning sentiment. Because of the way we use language, its nuances can be hard enough for humans to grasp, especially given that so little of true communication is verbal. It may be possible for a machine to detect changes in tone of voice and body temperature as indicators of arousal. However, determining whether such arousal is a result of stress or pleasure, for example, requires a far more sophisticated assessment that we humans take our lifetimes to refine—and even then we may get it wrong. Criminal trial in many countries is still by jury for the very same reason: humans are better at discerning a person's intention, and a computer is better at determining whether a ball is in or out on a tennis court.

There are, of course, scenarios in which sentiment is of no consequence in a legal process. Take for example the renewal of a driving license: regulations prescribe the information and documentation to be provided and the process through which they must flow in order for renewal to take place. The client journey is absolutely defined and there may be no deviation; this may be nerve-wracking for the applicant, but the attitude or sentiment of the individual are of no consequence or influence. That is not to say that there is no service opportunity, because there may be those who would like help to make sure they get the forms right and who don't feel confident dealing with applications online. Such support requires little in the way of specialist skills but a good deal of empathy and hand-holding. There are, however, many "open" situations in which sentiment is a key driver in decision-making and has a direct bearing on the way in which a matter proceeds, and therefore on potential outcomes.

I have wondered whether the next step in AT in relation to the law might be the presentation of potential courses of action (with associated stages, timelines, requirements, costs, and so on) based on simplified sentiment categories. I can imagine categories for disputes ranging from "Vindictive pursuit of retribution at any cost" to "I hate conflict so get me out of this at any cost"; I vividly recall one client who told me he wanted a lawyer that "eats nails and spits out battleships," who definitely fell in to the former category.

I may be underestimating the competence of legal tech hackers to encompass the vicissitudes of personal and business life and the multiplicity

of our reactions and responses to events. Perhaps this is because I hold to the vanity that we are far too complex and what drives us is largely hidden even from us in our subconscious. It is doubtless true that we can be directed towards certain choices, and the anticipation and influencing of our choices is what drives the development of assistive technologies by businesses that need to monetize their access to our attention. There is
perhaps a place for legal AT. I'd love to be involved in exploring what is possible.

THE FIVE PS

Some years ago in the course of a consulting project, I created a simple model in order to explain a proposition that has relevance here. My proposition is that clients go to a lawyer for Profit, Protection, Principle, or a combination of those three; what they Pay for is the lawyer's Power to deliver those outcomes. Clients in my experience seek outcomes that support their emotional needs as much as, if not more than, their rational objectives. Even a corporate client will invariably have a personal stake in a matter, as the outcome may well impact career progression and job security. Like it or not, underlying feelings are primary drivers of our responses to situations because they directly influence our thinking; they give energy to the beliefs that, in turn, underpin our attitudes.

A consultant with many years of experience advising veterinary practices told me that vets laboured under the fundamental misconception that all they had to do to be good vets was to administer to animals. In practice, their greatest challenge was not in treating animals but rather in dealing with the owners. A parallel can be drawn with young lawyers who bounce into practice full of their knowledge of the law and itching to apply it to interesting cases. What they find is that the skills they must develop and refine are in dealing with clients, who are the "owners" of what for them are significant life and business situations.

THE IMPORTANCE OF STORY

In his book *Sapiens: A Brief History of Humankind* Yuval Noah Harari proposes that we humans are separated from other animals by our ability to contrive and believe in fictions, such as myths and other constructs of our imagination. Storytelling suggests campfires and bedtime with children, yet it also underpins "oral tradition," which continues to this day as a means of passing on cultural and historical information. We are engrossed in stories every waking moment that form our ideas of ourselves and our place in the world. The "story of me" is the one that most absorbs us, and some propose that our sense of self relies entirely on our ability to recall the information that makes up our identity and that allows us to function in the world. If that recall becomes confused or defective, the consequences can be anything from mildly embarrassing to catastrophic.

Situations that arise in our personal and business lives are viewed according to the contextual background in which they occur, namely the storyline that we continuously construct that is the "story of me" and its various sub-plots. Our story follows the timeline of our life experiences and includes projected futures. Our storytelling is not a simple recital of facts about the past and suppositions about the future but is charged with ideas that determine how we feel about ourselves from moment to moment, from day to day. When clients come to you for help, they first and foremost want to know how the future might play out so as to ensure that they come out of it well, or at least with a minimum of collateral damage to their sense of self.

A really good lawyer has the ability to discern and address a client's needs on multiple levels. Key to most of us is the avoidance of shame, and it is important to acknowledge that vulnerability while at the same time respecting the social boundaries that make it difficult to discuss such matters openly. We know the value of rationality and must at the same time accommodate emotionality; client service involves the application of IQ and EQ.

I hope that by now I have made clear that there are profoundly human factors that influence client choices, which we are uniquely equipped to perceive and work with in our service to clients. Intelligence was once defined to me as a combination of intellect and sensitivity. Artificial Intelligence has a very long way to go before it can hope to master the nuances of human nature. A lawyer's skills in regard to the law and legal practice are a given; the real area of differentiation and advantage that is becoming ever more important is that of relationship.

Though I admit to being enthralled by innovation and many of the new technologies, I am not pretending to know which is likely to provide competitive advantage or enhance business process management. My interest is relationships and how we conduct them. Application program interfaces (APIs) are said to be the key to future app development because they are what makes it possible to pass information between apps; they are perhaps a metaphor for our human relationships, which are also made more productive and rewarding when information passes easily between us. Augmented reality is most valuable if it serves to augment relationships; many of the sharing technologies can be used to create a richer service experience for clients. They deserve our attention because they are capable of being more than fads for teenagers and "tech geeks."

Summary

- 'Artificial intelligence' (AI) as experienced today, and expected in the coming 5 years at least, is better described as 'Assistive Technology' (AT) which has a useful but limited role in legal services

- AI is not going to replace lawyers for a very long time, if ever, though it can and should support mutual understanding and meaningful exchange in professional service relationships

- AT is doing away with the most mechanical tasks and at the same time creating new roles and opportunities to impact client on-boarding and service experience

- Technology is not yet able to discern sentiment to any material degree and is certainly a long way from being able to work with the nuances of human emotionality

- Complex client situations give rise to complex responses and decision-making is influenced, to one degree or another, by individual feelings and interests that are seldom directly expressed or easily discerned

- Intelligence is the combination of intellect with sensitivity and we humans are uniquely placed to perceive and articulate genuine understanding of client needs

- In a fast evolving and competitive legal sector, the primary area of differentiation and advantage is that of relationship

3

Our Human Condition

We became more of a "business" than a human community.
Why should it be so surprising that being a human community
hinges on understanding humanness?
—*Greg Merten*

We are taught so much about the world around us and so
little about the world within us, just as, in the world of
science, we know so much about the solar system and so
little about what goes on inside our own planet Earth. We
are made up of body, mind, and spirit, yet know so little of
their capacities and interrelationships; we put fuel in, turn the
ignition, and drive. Along the way, we may stop from time to
time, out of choice or necessity, and come to learn something
more. Unfortunately, these tend to be times of crisis and
suffering—although we need not wait until then to learn
about our human condition.

I believe that the principles covered in this chapter and
the next should be taught in schools. Understanding and
working with our human condition is an essential life skill, a

foundation for establishing meaning and purpose and thereby leading a full life. I have been fortunate to learn, through study and from great teachers, principles that are fundamental to human experience and profoundly liberating. Instead of being blown along by time and tide, developing a fuller inner life enriches our experience and appreciation of all of life.

Lawyers are human first, lawyer second. Understanding the human condition is an essential life skill for lawyers, for their own benefit and for the benefit of others. What follows is not specific to lawyers but written with lawyers very much in mind. Where I suggest specific methods, it is because I have tried them and found them useful. I offer perspectives from which I have benefited, not specific prescriptions for personal career success, happiness, or fulfilment, as such matters are for each of us to find for ourselves.

What is essential is to want to know yourself better so that you can have the fullest possible experience of being you. Stripping back everything else, what we are is our capacity to experience—in every sense, through all our senses and through our self-reflective awareness. Living our own lives deliberately and intensely is life's singular opportunity to be pursued and relished.

CONSCIOUSNESS

The wonderful thing about consciousness is that it is one thing of which we can each be absolutely certain—and yet which science cannot explain. It is, in every sense, our very personal domain.

Our self-awareness, our self-reflective consciousness, as we experience it today, is thought to be a relatively recent development in the evolution of humankind. It may only be a matter of a few tens of thousands of years (Yuval Noah Harari, in his book *Sapiens: A Brief History of Humankind*, refers to a "cognitive revolution" that he says took place 70,000 years ago) since people began to realize that they could deliberately manipulate thoughts to form new ideas and perceptions. It has been suggested that language was the catalyst because it allowed people to learn from the experiences of others and to engage in structured thought by using language internally.

> *"An entirely new dimension had been added to our consciousness: verbal thought. We could form concepts, entertain ideas, appreciate patterns in events, apply reason, and begin to understand the universe in which we found ourselves."*
>
> —*Peter Russell, From Science to God*

From this self-awareness comes the capacity for individuation, the process by which we can explore and express our individuality and pursue personal goals. This capacity, however, gives rise to its own problems: the contortions and distortions of the ego.

Understanding the nature of consciousness is an essential foundation for self-management. Consciousness is our most precious and most powerful gift; to get back to the source of our experience, to its essential workings, is to know that we are free to choose how we experience our life and how we choose to interpret our life situations.

PERCEPTION

Our consciousness allows us to form perceptions that serve to characterize particular circumstances, situations, people, and things as broadly good or bad—or some combination of the two. We are constantly engaged in constructing and furnishing our relationship with the world around us and, therefore, the world within us. When we see something with our eyes, what we perceive is really a projection of that thing into our mind. The eighteenth century German philosopher Immanuel Kant drew the distinction between "phenomenon"—what we see in our mind—and "noumenon"—the thing itself. Indeed, all the input from our senses is necessarily experienced internally. Although there are many experiences that we could be said to share because we describe them similarly, each individual's perceptions are necessarily distinct.

Our perceptions directly engage the self. The self provides our point of view: the point from which we view. The way we see things is also influenced by the view that we have of ourselves. What helped me to understand this better was taking classes in perspective drawing; I did not become proficient in the slightest, but it helped me gain an understanding that has proved useful. For the drawing of an object to be an accurate representation, it must be drawn as it is and as you see it. In the same way, it is possible and desirable to see a set of circumstances as it is—from many angles—and then choose which view or perspective you will take of it.

This may seem rather complicated, yet I recommend you give it some attention and reflection. An understanding of this essential aspect of the human condition leads to discovering a means by which each of us can choose, for our own good and the good of others, to change the view we take of things so as to release our capacities for creativity, passion, and joy in our work and relationships.

The perceptions we construct are the result of accumulated personal experience and what we have learned from others. We have the capacity to take charge of our perceptions and to change them. We are not merely observers and learners; we are creators. Each of us has experiences of the reality outside of ourselves that are known only internally. The fact that others appear to share the same experiences can be reassuring but need not be limiting.

There are certain practical aspects to our humanity that we generally accept to be immutable: that gravity affects us, that skin will burn if placed in a naked flame, that we will eventually die. These and so many other "facts" are revealed to us as we pass through life. However, these facts do not preoccupy our thoughts, shape our personalities, or influence our relationships with others or with ourselves.

What preoccupies us are our perceptions of fear and love—our inner reality and our inner duality. The simplest binary model is that of love and fear: love is the willingness to include something or someone in our life, what we embrace and move towards (unconditional love being love without conditions for inclusion); fear is what we want to exclude and what we move away from.

Our tendency is to believe that we live in a world in which fear and behaviour driven by fear predominate and in which love is a scarcity; because that is what we believe, it is what we create. Our thoughts are propelled by our feelings and our feelings are propelled and elaborated by our thoughts. Other than in cases of instinctual reaction, our actions emerge from our thoughts and feelings. In fact, thoughts are actions themselves. If there were Thought Police, we might all be imprisoned; of course, we are already imprisoned by the resentments we hold towards others and, most importantly, towards ourselves; our inner critic is ever vigilant!

We have within each of us a thinker and a prover: the thinker thinks and the prover proves. If we think something is so, then we will gather all available evidence to confirm that what we think is true. In this way, if we fear something, our actions can bring about the very thing we fear. We are so accustomed to living in a state of fear and experiencing the stress it produces in us that we become adapted, or rather, maladapted, to this state, which in turn governs our attitude and our direction in life.

Respiration is part of our autonomic nervous system. Breathing is automatic and does not require our conscious involvement. However, we can consciously intervene to change our respiration. In the same way, we have the capacity to consciously intervene to change our perceptions. Very few of us have the opportunity to learn of the benefits that may be obtained from careful and measured intervention to change our breathing; equally few intervene in their own thought processes to choose a different view of things. Working with our breath and our perceptions to enhance our life experience and well-being are life skills that we can all learn and practice.

Just as we can choose to breathe differently in order to induce physiological and psychological benefits, we can intervene to change our perceptions; we can choose to perceive things differently. It is disconcerting to think that our individual stories, our so carefully elaborated identities, can be so easily reconceived. A sense of self based in fear is one we fear to relinquish.

GETTING TO KNOW "ME"

We are told that we should know ourselves. I was for a long time confounded by the injunction "know thyself" because I thought it required me to know all my preferences, likes, dislikes, qualities, and vices—all of the apparent and secret facets of my identity. I was never clear what benefit that would bring and whether I could ever complete the task and so left it on my "to do" list.

I now realize that to know yourself is really an opportunity to come to know that part of your consciousness that is not part of your identity, that has the capacity for awareness and to act as a witness to the workings of your mind. This self is often called the "higher self"; higher perhaps because it is above the turmoil of our "little self." Both of these selves operate within us and can work together for our benefit. Learning how to do this deliberately, consciously, is a first step towards self-management.

One means by which you can come to know your higher self, your witness, is through meditation, which teaches how to still the mind by the simple device of noticing its activity. To notice the stream of thoughts that come and go is to establish a place of awareness from which that noticing occurs. This creates a new dynamic, a new perspective or point of view from which to see things differently. If you can see things differently, then you can make a choice between a perception that is shaped by fear and one that is not. Perception becomes a creative process in which we have read and write privileges.

> *"If you change the way you look at things, the things you look at will change."*
> —Wayne Dyer, *Manifest Your Destiny*

Our little self, also called our "egoic" self, is the one caught up in our identity—the story of "me" (the "me" in *meaning*). This story is the one we tell when we are asked to "say something" about ourselves. We begin with our name, line of work, marital status, offspring, and so on. We describe our social identity and, if encouraged, tell some of the story of "me": the circumstances with which we identify and from which we daily elaborate our identity.

When we think we are relating to others, we are often telling (and perhaps listening) to our respective rehearsed stories. Similarly, our relationships with others can be seen as the "stories so far" of our interactions. In dealing with others, it is extremely difficult to disengage our own identities—to stop evaluating what we hear in terms of how it affects us or what aspects of our experience it triggers in memory. We are steeped in stories, in our individual and collective "oral traditions," as a means of expressing ourselves and sharing knowledge.

A mental model I find useful is the Matryoshka or Russian nested wooden doll. As we grow up we crystallize identities, versions of "me," at various stages of our lives; although on the outside we look grown up, we are still holding all the earlier versions within us. These are layers of feelings (and associated thoughts) in which all past hurts are stored and can be reignited by even apparently trivial experiences. The egoic self is the protector against hurts and can summon the full force of unreconciled feelings to colour our perceptions. Like a loving relative trying to protect you from harm, the egoic self has the best intentions but can be stifling if you only listen to its warning voice.

We are at times encouraged to take a "leap of faith," and I have spent considerable time wondering where we are leaping from. In the end, I concluded that we leap from the imagined precipice created by the egoic self in order to fulfil its prime directive to protect us from risking change to our sense of self.

Self-management does not mean suppressing the egoic self but learning to live in harmony with it as part of your make up, part of your humanity; what David Hawkins called "domesticating the ego." It also means allowing another intelligence to emerge, one that engages the whole capacity and reach of your consciousness.

SELF-WORTH

Our relationships define us; we are constantly engaged in constructing our identities based on our perceptions and experiences of those relationships. We feel our way through the world each day by "pinging" others with our social sonar to establish our position in our inner space. There is no problem that is not, at one level or another, a relationship problem. There are few joys that are not based in or shared through relationships.

It has been said that every human action can be put down to the avoidance of shame and that shame is the lowest form of human experience. In mythology, and in history, banishment is the epitome of shame because it means complete exclusion from the social family. It has also been said that our main drives are to be safe; to have approval (so that we are safe); and to have control (so that we are assured approval). There is in most of us a longing to be included and accepted in whatever group we identify with.

We admire and are naturally drawn to those who appear to have a strong sense of self-worth. Our own self-worth is constantly tested and all too easily undermined if not grounded in something more enduring and meaningful than our fragile social identity. Lack of self-worth is the root of insecurity, fear, and alienation of others. Establishing a sound basis for self-worth can begin with recognition of our shared human condition.

Unfortunately, huge efforts are made to persuade us that self-worth equates to financial worth (the "he who dies with the most toys wins" model). We are conditioned to want an ever-increasing and more diverse array of accessories that will make us more desirable to others and in some way enhance our quality of life. We are often preoccupied with getting things, while at the same time we know that the best things in life are not things. Exploring the domain of your own consciousness leads to the discovery that real power is the power to do without things.

I have a rule that I never envy people for what they have (or appear to have). If I think I should have what someone else has, then I remember that to have what I want of his, I would have to take *all* of what he has and is—and therefore be him. I don't want to be anyone else; I want to be me. Therefore, envy is not an option. Someone wisely said to me once: "Jealousy—never let it in your life." When someone has something that you believe you would enjoy if you had it, then be genuinely happy for that person and share in his or her experience of whatever good it brings. As Will Smith's character says to Kevin James's character in the movie *Hitch*: "You do you and I'll do me."

The struggle to improve our circumstances can mean that as our material wealth increases, our spiritual poverty increases. (This does not necessarily work the other way around—although don't try to persuade a committed ascetic of that.) As always, there is a balance to be struck. Material things are not intrinsically bad or wrong any more than nature is good or evil. However, it is our spirituality, or, in other words, our consciousness, that is the only channel of experience and the only means by which we can truly secure for ourselves the well-being and self-worth we thrive on.

Where does true self-worth lie? Well, the answer is in your own experience. Only you can know what qualities of thought, action, and experience evoke in you a profound and enduring sense of harmony and well-being. These qualities may include kindness, appreciation, perseverance, creativity, advocacy, and silence (all of which are valued in lawyers, incidentally).

SCARCITY

We are conditioned socially to believe in, and so create, scarcity. The scarcity principle holds that there will not be enough for everyone and so not enough for you: not enough money, not enough love, not enough places at the table. So you must strive to have more and to store and protect what you collect. It is the belief that has people lining up for gasoline at 2 a.m. because there is a possibility of a shortage that is thereby created or exacerbated.

The scarcity principle is the tool of marketing and compliance professionals and what fuels the madness that overcomes people on the first day of retail sales. Things become desirable because they are scarce and, at one level, we believe that if we have them then we are somehow also more desirable. Wanting more things and more money to get more things is a sure sign that there is something else lacking.

This subject brings to mind a greeting card I once saw (decorated with pictures of jewellery and clothing) that said, "The difference between us and other animals is that we can accessorize." As we know, the initial exhilaration and sense of power fades all too quickly. It is well established that those who have wealth generally never tire of acquiring more—another image springs to my mind of a billboard advertisement depicting a hamster running in a bejewelled hamster wheel.

The trap set by having more is that it almost immediately activates the fear of losing it. Winning the lottery often reveals the suffering that great wealth can bring; many who win find their lives and, most importantly, their relationships changed forever—for the worse. The idea of a thing is invariably more beguiling, and more rewarding in the sense of the imagined pleasure it engenders, than the experience of the thing.

The very best antidote to the influence of scarcity is a practice of gratitude. Remembering and enumerating all we have to be grateful for is the best guarantee of discharging the depleting and self-diminishing and destructive force of a scarcity mindset. When I choose to think of what I am grateful for, I find that it is relationships more than objects. It is in what you truly value that you find the foundations of self-worth. A businessman I met once told me that he was asked what he would give his life for. He answered that he would give his life for his children, and it was suggested to him that he would indeed do well to devote his life to those he valued most.

Evolving within yourself a sense of self-worth allows you to find the power to do without things, which ensures that things have no power over you. You may then choose more effectively among objects, recognizing their true value and purpose; you need never again squander your precious energy on what can never improve your quality of life. In choosing to pursue a material goal, stop to ask, "What do I believe this will bring me?" When an answer emerges, ask the question again. Ask the question of each answer that comes up to get at the root of what you expect.

I was once introduced to a partner in a provincial firm who told me, "We want to grow our firm." I asked why, and he answered, "So we can make more money." I asked why, and he said, "So we can pay ourselves more money." I asked why. He stopped for a moment and said, "We should talk."

CONTROL

It is the deep-seated vanity of each of us, of our egoic self, that we believe we can so engineer our circumstances and so control our relationships as to bring about security and certainty. Instead, we have to learn how to deal with things as they are rather than as we wish they would be; while old habits die hard, new ways can bring immense reward. So long as you resist things as they are, you are draining yourself of energy; as soon as you are able to accept things as they are, then your energy can be directed. You may put that effort toward changing how things are (perhaps starting with the view you take of things).

One of the reasons that we come to believe that we are somehow in control is the multitude of set behaviours that make up our social infrastructure. These are dance steps and routines with well-defined parameters. They are like the uniform measure of time we set our clocks by: they are real in the sense that they have wide-ranging effects, and yet they have little to do with our essential consciousness. They keep us busy. They keep us involved. They keep us playing the part we were trained to play. They too easily keep us from ourselves and from others. They form the intricate web of what Harari calls "imagined order."

There was a time, when I used to fly on business a great deal, when I would hold on tightly to the arm rests and concentrate fiercely on the movement of the aircraft whenever we moved through turbulence. When I thought about it, I realized that at some level I believed that by concentrating I was somehow keeping the aircraft on course and in the air. I was not doing it because I feared being thrown from my seat. Such vanity! It is no different when I try to make things turn out the way I would like or have others do as I wish them to.

Everything of any importance to me in my life is concerned in one way or another with relationships. My aspirations invariably involve other people and their participation in events as I wish them to unfold. I have to remind myself constantly that I also have a part to play in achieving their aspirations and that they too wish me to behave and act in particular ways, according to *their* desired version of the future. The only chance any of us has to have things turn out closer to what we wish is to expressly engage the consent of others.

In Buddhist teaching, the principal cause of suffering is said to be attachment: attachment to things, outcomes, people, and perceptions. This is another way of referring to our innate desire to have things the way we wish them to be. Relaxing our hold on the arm rests, letting go of our grip on that over which we have no control, relieves us from the stress of flying the aircraft from our passenger seat.

Attachment to negative perceptions and the emotions that accompany them is a major drain on our energies. Release is obtained through forgiveness. To forgive is to "let go" and applies specifically to the perceptions we have constructed of the past and its events. Forgiveness is good for you. Anger, and the guilt that lies beneath it, can be so easily diffused by the simple conscious decision to choose the opportunities that this moment presents over those you believe you lost in the past or will not have in the future. It is all too easy to be miserable about what was or what might have been—and to project that story into a future in which you prove yourself right.

We can choose to let go of the frisson we obtain from being "the one who was wronged." When circumstances are not as I want, I ask myself, "How does this serve my purpose?" The flippant answer is that it doesn't. I then have to look to another part of myself, usually hiding in plain sight, that sees some advantage, however at odds with what I think I want, in things being as they are. I have to bring that part to the fore and negotiate. It isn't a comfortable process; however, it gets results.

There are occasions when a drastic change in environment and circumstances are needed. Yet whatever your environment or circumstances, you will still be there, applying your same learned perceptions to new situations to reinforce your sense of self and your beliefs. Most of the time, however, a change of attitude is all that is needed: starting with an attitude of gratitude. To change the way you see something is to change that thing in the most important way for you. When you make that change within you, the other is also changed.

VULNERABILITY

Something lawyers encounter a great deal is vulnerability. Clients, however powerful or forceful they may appear, are all vulnerable in one way or another, if only to the consequences of not achieving the outcomes they desire. Being wrong, losing face, and failing are all examples of what the ego seeks to avoid as these outcomes bring with them the dread of shame. We can and should be sensitive to the vulnerabilities of clients and colleagues in legal practice and be wary of the opportunity we have to abuse the power we may have over others who entrust us with their vulnerability.

In intimate relationships such as marriage, perhaps the most precious gift we can give and receive is our vulnerability. We can all too easily vent our frustration and sense of powerlessness by exercising the power to be hurtful to our partner. In an organization such as a law practice, there needs to be a great deal of trust among partners and among staff if the organization is not to become a place of friction and fear. Junior staff are vulnerable to the slightest negativity expressed by those in authority, and even partners can fear the consequences of being singled out for criticism.

PAST, FUTURE, PRESENT

What makes our human consciousness special is that we have the capacity to record and analyse the past as well as construct and evaluate potential futures.

In most of us, this takes up just about all our processing capacity as we seek to reinvent the past and pre-invent the future. Very little attention is given to the present moment unless there is something truly extraordinary that captures our attention to such an extent that we briefly suspend our processing of past and future. These are moments that all of us have experienced at one time or another and can recognize as moments of well-being.

Most of us occupy our available cognitive capacity in any given moment with thoughts of the past and thoughts of the future. Our thoughts of the past may be rehearsed in an attempt to understand what the past means to us and to help us formulate a view of the future in the context of some anticipated event or ongoing relationship. Attached to and embedded within all such thoughts is the story of "me." We are preoccupied by thoughts that relate to the view we take of things and what impact those things will have upon our egoic selves, which we have been so meticulously building since we first became aware of ourselves as individuals.

What we can do instead is bring our consciousness, our attention, to bear in the present moment. We can bring compassion, kindness, meaning, and purpose to each moment, particularly each moment of relating with others, through a conscious choice to give our attention fully to what is happening now. We can consciously choose present-moment awareness as a means of intervention to dispel fruitless preoccupation with the past and future. We can use this moment to promote love (inclusion) instead of fear (exclusion).

There is only one context in which any of us can experience intuition, obtain insight, and experience anything; that is the present. The present moment is the only time in which you can give your attention to anyone or anything. It is the only time in which you can listen, make a decision, or take action. It is, indeed, all there is, and yet to refer to it as "time" is to suggest that it is somehow limited by the linear march of clock time. The present moment is far better thought of as a space or a context within which we may have conscious experience.

The present moment is only fully accessible and experienced through self-awareness. Self-awareness involves the capacity to bring attention in any given moment to your state of mind, your feelings, your body, and your overall state of being. Self-awareness is the starting point for recognizing and discerning the difference between things as we perceive them and as they might be if we were to perceive them differently. Far from being an esoteric practice, self-awareness and the useful direction of energy and attention has always been central to success in business life.

Learning how to collect yourself and to bring yourself into present-moment awareness is essential if you are to learn to see things as they are rather than as you fear them to be. Though there may be specific circumstances and places in which you feel most able to calm yourself, the calm is actually occurring internally and, though it may be engaged or undermined by external circumstances, the only space in which you can feel calm is within. Life as a legal professional is simply too demanding and too potentially stressful not to learn how to collect yourself in the present moment in order to find balance, calm, and clarity of mind.

FLOW

Psychologist and author Mihaly Csikszentmihalyi has reported on decades of research into happiness and what he calls "optimal" or "flow" experiences. A flow experience is one that occurs when an individual is engaged in an activity in which the challenges involved are within a certain tolerance of the individual's skills required to meet them. Activity in which the challenges lie beneath a person's level of skills is likely to induce boredom; activity in which the challenges are well beyond that level of skills is likely to induce anxiety. The "flow channel" represents the notional space, or tolerance, within which an individual can have a complex experience.

A flow experience leaves the self more complex than before and such complexity is what we commonly refer to as personal growth. As Csikszentmihalyi says in his book *Flow*:

> Complexity is the result of two broad psychological processes: differentiation and integration. Differentiation implies a movement towards uniqueness, toward separating oneself from others. Integration refers to its opposite: a union with other people, with ideas and entities beyond the self.

Borrowing from this description, we can think of fear as differentiation and love as integration.

Having fun does not mean that we are not challenged, tested, and asked to stretch ourselves. Having fun is not easy—in the sense that doing what is easy does not of itself allow us to have fun. Our ideas about what might be fun are often the product of suggestion and fantasy, and that's what ideas should be; however, we can all too often be ill-prepared, find ourselves ill-equipped, or simply make ourselves ill when we try to pursue them.

Good fun is good for you *and* good for others. Having fun at the expense of others is no more than selfish indulgence and excluding others leads to separation and alienation. Having fun is about growing and sharing; it is a way of being loving towards yourself and towards others.

A flow experience is what lawyers mean when they talk about "having fun" in the context of their practices. Although we can talk about it, what constitutes "fun" will always be an essentially individual experience (as it should be, for reasons I explain later in this chapter) and one that is relevant at a specific time and may prove true for that time only. We know when we are having fun and can tell stories about when we had fun; we also quickly recognize within ourselves when we are not having fun. We are conditioned not to expect to have fun all the time—or perhaps seldom—and to accept that for the rest of the time we must be satisfied with the rewards of duty. For much of the time, most lawyers are not having fun in the sense of finding "flow."

Understanding these principles allows lawyers to consider the balance between challenges and skills for themselves and for those they manage. Lawyers need to be fair to themselves and to others when it comes to accepting and delegating work. Biting off more than you can chew is not good for you and not good for me. There is no benefit in accepting or imposing tasks that cause too much anxiety. Knowing your own and others' limitations is the first step in discovering how best to reach beyond them.

We cannot always have work that stretches us to just the right degree and projects that present fresh challenges at just the right increments. A lot of what lawyers do appears repetitive. However, flow is still to be found by looking beyond routine and finding challenges elsewhere: finding more efficient ways of working alone and with colleagues, taking notice and care of the client experience, delivering greater value in terms of presentation, learning from others.

AUTOTELIC EXPERIENCE

The term *autotelic* comes from the Greek *auto*, meaning "self," and *telos*, meaning "goal." Csikszentmihalyi (a Hungarian name that is apparently pronounced "cheeks sent me high") uses this term to describe the situation in which any activity becomes intrinsically rewarding—an experience in which an individual gives attention to an activity for its own sake rather than focusing on its consequences. In other words, you do it because it feels good and you are doing it for you.

Activities undertaken in service of others, out of duty, because we are compelled to do them, or because we expect some future benefit from them are said to be "exotelic." Most activities are neither purely autotelic nor exotelic. The practice of law is one in which exotelic activities predominate. The opportunity is to discover the autotelic value and enjoy the concurrent pleasure of the moment.

Csikszentmihalyi writes:

> The autotelic experience, or flow, lifts the course of life to a different level. Alienation gives way to involvement, enjoyment replaces boredom, helplessness turns into a feeling of control, and psychic energy works to reinforce the sense of self, instead of being lost in the service of external goals. When experience is intrinsically rewarding life is justified in the present, instead of being held hostage to a hypothetical future gain.

For the lawyer, experience is either predominantly document-based or relationship-based. Research and drafting are the only purely document-based activities, and even those are relationship-based. All else that a lawyer is involved in during daily practice directly involves relationships inside and outside the firm. If only for this reason, and if experience in these relationships is not to be entirely exotelic, there is rich ground for gaining optimal experience and thereby delivering optimal performance. Interactions with others need not be something to get through as quickly as possible so as to get onto the next thing; they present opportunities for learning, giving, and growing. Unfortunately, demands on time and the billable cost of time are constantly working against us and taking us out of "flow."

This brings us back again to the importance of giving attention to the present moment. Doing so does not mean that everything has to take twice as long. Your dealings with others can be just as economical in terms of time, and yet the quality of that time becomes wholly different if you give your full attention. Giving your full attention to the person with whom you are interacting means that your interaction is likely also to be considerably more effective.

THE LIMITATIONS OF ATTENTION

It is important to understand our limitations when it comes to our conscious mind. These are limits that we can work with, perhaps even work to stretch a little bit, or that can work against us.

We have only a limited amount of real-time conscious processing capacity. Research indicates that we can handle about seven pieces of information at any one time and this capacity could be described as our "attention span." This information is concerned with differentiation. First of all, we filter out much of what comes in through our senses and select for conscious examination those bits of information that are of particular interest or concern to us, whether in the form of threats or opportunities.

While there is clearly a vast amount of information being collected and processed, we can only deal with a very limited amount of it in our conscious mind. Like a computer with limited RAM (random access memory), we can only have a certain number of concurrent applications running at any one time without losing performance or causing a system crash. The important difference here is that our conscious mind is preoccupied with the impact that the new information has on the self: how we feel about ourselves, how others think of us, whether something reinforces or undermines our goals, and so on.

What happens to us all, and all too often, is that our conscious mind becomes disordered as a result of information coming in that interferes with our current intentions, threatening or interfering with the way we wish things to be. This disorder can take many forms, such as anger, fear, frustration, worry, and jealousy—all conditions that threaten or hurt the self. Whether justified or not, this disorder in consciousness directly affects our well-being. In the sixth century BC, Epictetus summed it up in this way: "People are not disturbed by things, but by the view they take of them."

Our thoughts whirl around, repeating and recycling the same information and our views of its impact on us. This is what is commonly called "worrying." While we are thinking in this way, we are bringing in nothing new because our processing capability is occupied with the same thoughts. This is panic, overload, and confusion, with no room for insight and creativity. However, we have the capacity to consciously intervene by choosing to see things differently, bringing new order to consciousness through a fresh intention to occupy our conscious attention span with what is useful and rewarding. I think of this as pressing the stop button on the "cracked record," and I often tell myself out loud to "Stop!" I have read that during our inner monologues, our tongues make tiny movements that are micro versions of what our tongue does when we speak aloud. If the record keeps on playing, you can take literally hold of your tongue while holding the idea STOP in your mind—one to try when you have some privacy, I suggest.

There is an important distinction to be made between attention and intention: attention is the direction of our conscious mind; intention is the direction of the whole of our intelligence, including our subconscious. To form an intention is to create space for something new to emerge; once present, you can give attention to it by thinking about it. Forming an intention to be still and to listen is achieved by inviting and allowing those conditions to arise; thinking about being still and listening is just that and no more. Intention directs your psychic energy to what is useful to the fulfilment of your intention.

THE LAWYER SELF

For the lawyer, in addition to all of the normal social conditioning, there are added the significant rigours and rules of legal professional practice. As lawyers we take on a whole raft of behavioural traits and expectations that we assimilate through our study of the law, our observations of more senior lawyers, and perceptions of our "role" in society. Benjamin Sells, a psychotherapist and former lawyer, in his book *The Soul of the Law*, addresses this area in great detail and depth. He reports that

> The primary psychological complaints among lawyers are interpersonal feelings of inadequacy and inferiority, anxiety, social alienation and isolation, and depression. The theme running through all of these symptoms is a lack of involvement and interest in the larger world beyond the law. Lawyers are being cut off from their sense of belonging to a broader community. This detachment appears variously as an inability to sustain intimate relationships, a feeling of social ostracism, destructive competitiveness, and bad manners.

A root cause of these complaints is, according to Sells, the fact that lawyers consider it their role to bring objectivity to everything and everyone they encounter, taking on the mantle of the archetype of the law itself. With a sword in one hand and scales in the other, how much more can we be expected to handle?

In the case of the lawyer, the fears of the egoic self are expanded and magnified far beyond what most deal with. Fears include fear of making a mistake, fear of what others will think of you if you do make a mistake, fear of not knowing what to do or what to say, fear of failure, fear of being publicly rebuked by our professional governing body or the court, and so on.

Needing to be right all of the time takes on a whole new dimension when you are a lawyer, knowing the ignominious consequences of being wrong and the delight that others will take in bringing you down. These fears can invade all instances of challenge to a lawyer regardless of the magnitude of the issue. Add to this the lawyer's propensity to look for flaws in any contrary position and you have a recipe for extreme defensive behaviour, familiar to anyone who has ever been involved in a legal negligence claim.

Pretty soon, if you are not careful, there are enemies everywhere and every situation carries the seeds of failure and fault. What happened to fun? You embraced the siege mentality that so many lawyers suffer from and as many cover up with bravura and posturing of one kind or another. This is one way that lawyers can lose themselves in their work, becoming isolated and untrusting, lonely and uncaring.

POSITIVE PSYCHOLOGY

American positive psychologist Martin E. P. Seligman, PhD, in his book *Authentic Happiness*, addresses the legal profession in his section, "Why Are Lawyers So Unhappy?" He reports that lawyers appear at the top of a list of 104 occupations in terms of major depressive disorder, suffering from depression at a rate that is 3.6 times higher than employed persons generally. Lawyers also have higher rates of alcoholism, illegal drug use, and divorce – "they are the best paid profession, and yet they are disproportionately unhappy and unhealthy." If this isn't true for you now, beware: it may yet touch your life when you least expect. Seligman goes on to say, "Lawyers are trained to be aggressive, judgemental, intellectual, analytical and emotionally detached. This produces predictable emotional consequences for the legal practitioner: he or she will be depressed, anxious and angry a lot of the time."

The answer, according to Seligman, is to identify the key drivers of this malaise and to then address them using positive psychology techniques that are tried and tested. These techniques are founded on the belief that we each have strengths on which we can build and through which we can find authenticity: our meaning and purpose.

Seligman and others undertook a study of major religious and philosophical traditions and came down to six virtues common to almost all:

1. Wisdom and knowledge
2. Courage
3. Love and humanity
4. Justice
5. Temperance
6. Spirituality and transcendence

Seligman lists twenty-four strengths that underpin these virtues whose exercise brings enduring gratification to the individual and provides the basis for a meaningful life.

Exercising these strengths and virtues requires acts of will. Positive psychology is predicated on the idea that we are able to choose how we view events and circumstances and how we direct our will. We can choose to see things differently; we can choose to think and act in ways conducive to our personal good and, as a happy cause and consequence, the good of others.

Of course, these rightly lauded virtues are not always accessible to us, especially when we are angry and fearful. In his book *A Small Treatise on the Great Virtues*, André Comte-Sponville begins with politeness, which, though not itself a virtue, is a proper resort when no virtues are available to you because it limits the harm that you might otherwise cause. Some people regard politeness as something old-fashioned and quaint in a world where we are encouraged to express our feelings and "tell it how it is." Politeness, particularly in professional life, is essential and should be embraced by all, however clever and powerful they may think they are.

Summary

- Working with our human nature (our psychological, physiological and spiritual predispositions and capacities) lies at the heart of self-management

- Our perceptions are projections within us and our experiences are shaped by the view we take of them

- We have the power to consciously intervene in the interpretation of events and their meaning for us in the context of stories we construct with regard to who we are, and how we are, in relationship to others

- We each have an 'egoic' self that has a predisposition towards fear and is so protective that it sees danger everywhere, causing stress in the face of situations that it is powerless to change

- An enduring sense of self-worth is better grounded in virtues and quality of experience rather than in things

- Real power is the power to do without things so that things do not hold power over you

- Control is illusory, especially when it comes to events and the actions of others, and our power instead lies in deciding how we choose to see them

- We are all vulnerable and do well to remember that when dealing with clients and colleagues alike if we are not to cause harm to relationships

- We can only observe and influence our present state, and that of others, by focusing our attention in the present moment

- Achieving optimal, or 'flow', experience involves deliberate engagement with what stretches us (to the right degree) and in pursuit of goals from we and others benefit

- Lawyers have very particular vulnerabilities that arise from their role in relation to the Law itself, as well as expectations self-imposed and placed on them in a highly competitive and often combative profession

- Exercise of core virtues brings enduring gratification to the individual and provides the basis for a meaningful life

- Politeness, though not a virtue, is essential and should be embraced by all, however clever or powerful

Body Matters

I have come to realize that for most of this life I was like the James Joyce character, Mr. Duffy: someone who "lived a short distance from his body." I took my body for granted and assumed it to have a secondary role in my life experience. I have used it for a good deal of work, sports, indulgence, and pleasure. I simply did not know how critical my physiological well-being is to my psychological well-being and vice versa. I have come to appreciate what was said by someone who was careful about what he ate: "If I don't look after my body, I'll have nowhere to live."

Self-management includes understanding and listening to your body, tuning in to the body's innate intelligence. If you think your body is just a casual bystander, think again. Every thought you generate, and the energy that follows it, is experienced within the whole of your body. The impact of psychology on physiology is well known; we have all heard the term *psychosomatic* without, perhaps, fully appreciating its meaning. "Psycho" refers to mind; "soma" refers to body.

Equally important are *somatopsychic* conditions: the impact of our physiology on our psychology. A hangover is one of the simple examples of the short-term after-effects of poisoning yourself for pleasure. The evidence shows that cognitive performance is physiologically underpinned. If you want to think straight, you have to have to pay attention to your body and work with it rather than against it. I am not going to recommend any particular exercise or dietary regime. Instead, I want to draw attention to some key body matters that I hope will inspire you to find out more.

There are three aspects of the integrity of the body that are of particular importance and of which every one of us should be aware if we are to take care of ourselves properly. These aspects are the intelligence of the heart, the importance of breath, and the pH balance of the body. Attentiveness to these aspects, if built into the practice of awareness, can contribute greatly to physical, mental, and spiritual well-being. As I have mentioned before, I use the term *spiritual* here in the sense of consciousness.

The concept of *integrity* is particularly important here. I have learned that body and mind and spirit are part of an intraoperative and cooperative whole. Just as it is possible for all to be in alignment with one another, in balance and harmony, it is common for one to intervene to the detriment of the others and so of the whole; conversely, beneficial intervention is also possible. Vanity would have us believe that our selves, our mind and learned identity, are in charge. Thankfully, that is not the case. Just as Mercedes intends to make driving safer by taking as many decisions as possible away from the driver; nature has also deemed it sensible to leave the extraordinarily complex operation of our bodies to the intelligence of the body itself.

HEART INTELLIGENCE

It has only been discovered relatively recently that the heart incorporates some 40,000 neurons and has other features similar to the brain; a whole new discipline of neurocardiology has sprung up only in the last 15 years. I also recently came across reference to "psychoneuroimmunology" as a form of diagnosis and treatment offered by a recognized health insurer that focuses on heart rate variability and its impact on our health and longevity. Reducing on average by 3 percent a year throughout life, heart rate variability (HRV) refers to the variance in the time between heartbeats, something that can only be measured electronically. The reduction in our heart rate variability is significantly accelerated by the effects of stress.

The heart has a direct line to the brain through the vagus nerve, which forms a feedback loop; activity or intervention commencing in either area is immediately communicated to the other. It seems that our hearts are a source of sense and sensitivity that forms part of our overall intelligence, as people have known since long before science came to measure it. The heart is a prime source of our intuition and emotional intelligence. As Pascal put it, "The heart has its reasons of which reason knows nothing."

The electrical output of the heart is 40 to 50 times greater than that of the brain. The electromagnetic output of the heart is as much as 5,000 times greater than that of the brain and can be measured at a considerable distance from the body. Research has shown that the heart responds in preparation for stimulus several seconds before that stimulus appears so that it can be perceived intellectually. The heart "knows" before our minds do.

In his book *Influence: Science and Practice*, the renowned psychologist Robert B. Cialdini writes about what he calls "heart-of-heart signs" as a means of discerning whether we have been deliberately caught out by predisposition to act in consistency with prior commitment decisions. To recognize and resist the undue influence of consistency pressures on our compliance decisions, he says, we should "listen for signals coming from two places within us: our stomachs and our heart of hearts." Here Cialdini is also referring to what many of us know as a "gut" feeling. Science has demonstrated that neurons are also found throughout the entire gastrointestinal system, forming what is now referred to as the enteric nervous system.

The heart develops before the brain in the human body. When a heart is transplanted, it is capable of continuing to operate independently despite the fact that connections to the brain have not been made; though they may reconnect over time, it is not necessary for the functioning of the heart. The notion of an independent heart "brain" is further reinforced by the study of transplant patients who acquire tastes and in some cases even have memories that turn out to be associated with the donor.

Research carried out by the HeartMath Institute in the United States over the past 15 years has led to the development of proven techniques for heart-based intervention that have a dramatic influence on the consequences of stress and the improvement of intellectual capacity or "cortical facilitation." HeartMath discovered that when the electrical output of the heart goes to .1 hertz, then the rest of the autonomic nervous system also moves towards .1 hertz. Measurements of the brain's alpha waves show a similar movement towards the level of .1 hertz. This alignment of body and brain functions is known as *entrainment*, a term used to describe, for example, the synchronous movements of flocks of birds.

What has also been identified is that when the heart's electrical output moves to .1 hertz, HRV also becomes what is known as "coherent." When viewed over a period of time, visible in a matter of minutes using the right technology, a state of coherence can be seen to produce a regular sine wave pattern. A state of incoherence brought on, for example, by frustration or anger, produces by comparison an erratic and jagged pattern, contrasting very obviously with the flow and balance of the state of coherence. We can learn to quickly bring about coherence using a simple breathing technique; this involves breathing in for five seconds and out for five seconds. (It turns out that counting to ten really does help.) This coherence is reinforced and enhanced by evoking a positive experience, which, as far as the body is concerned, is indistinguishable from the experience itself.

The power of visualization is used extensively in sports and executive coaching. In his book *Coaching for Performance*, Sir John Whitmore reports that the javelin thrower Steve Backley was able to dramatically reduce his recovery time following a shoulder operation by visualizing his usual training sessions. Sports psychologists teach athletes to place themselves mentally "in the event," thereby preparing their responses for the actual experience. Positive affirmation is then used as a trigger for positive emotions and perception. This "self-talk" or self-coaching is a powerful means by which the mind can allow the body to perform freely and to its capacity. The "inner game" is one that has as much application for lawyers in professional life as it does for sportsmen.

For the lawyer, there are many possible applications of this technique: visualizing your meeting with a client being productive and convivial, seeing yourself dealing confidently with an old file you have been putting off for weeks, reassuring yourself that you are an experienced advocate and that you think very well "on your feet," visualizing yourself meeting new people and enjoying the company of old contacts at a conference, seeing yourself renewing a respectful relationship with your assistant. Try it, wholeheartedly, and see how often things turn out as well as you imagined.

NEUROGENESIS

Until recently, I thought that after our teenage years passed our neurons begin to die off and that this was an inescapable fact of life in an aging body. Not so, it seems. Neurogenesis, the creation of new neurons, continues—provided we do our part to encourage that process.

In a fascinating TED talk titled "You Can Grow New Brain Cells: Here's How," Dr. Sandrine Thuret, PhD, Principal Investigator and Lecturer in Neural Stem Cell Research at King's College London, tells of her research in this field and the lifestyle choices that support neurogenesis.

Dr. Thuret points to a number of dietary choices that promote neurogenesis, such as consumption of flavonoids (found in dark chocolate, blueberries, and other fruits and vegetables) and omega-3 fatty acids (found in salmon and other fishes). Dietary practices such as calorie restriction of 20 to 30 percent and intermittent fasting are also beneficial. Choices that are detrimental include high-fat diets and alcohol (although red wine is said to have some benefits, in moderation). Behavioural factors, such as learning, also help neurogenesis; sleep deprivation and stress are detrimental.

The research also shows that exercise produces dramatically greater levels of neurogenesis in mice with running wheels in their cages than those without. So, while you may, dear reader, be working very hard in pursuit of your career, make sure you use your bejewelled hamster wheel regularly!

BREATHING

We all know that breathing is essential to life. We certainly know what it feels like to be short of breath, such as when we run for a bus or walk up a long flight of stairs. Most of us don't realize that we often hold our breath in moments of concentration and anxiety. For those who like to jog, establishing a comfortable breathing rate will be familiar. Those who take sports seriously soon learn what aerobic and anaerobic activities feel like. We tend to associate awareness of breathing with deliberate physical activity. Otherwise, breathing takes care of itself and we do not consciously intervene to regulate our breath as we go through the day.

What has been known for some 5,000 years and confirmed by modern science is that our breathing has far-reaching effects on our health, our capacity to think and act, and our general sense of well-being. Breathing affects our cortical functions, metabolism, nervous, endocrine, and immune systems. Breathing is not just essential to life; it has a direct impact on quality of life and life experience. I hope that these are reasons enough to regard breathing as something worth knowing a little more about.

When we breathe, we bring in oxygen and expel carbon dioxide. The purpose is to oxygenate the blood and drive our metabolism; oxygen is absorbed into the blood and transported to the cells, which then take in the oxygen and expel carbon dioxide, which is transported back to the lungs to be disposed of during exhalation.

Rhythmical respiration has been known for a very long time to be a source of balance for body, mind, and spirit. If you are unaware of your breathing and feeling stress, then you will likely breathe inefficiently and inadequately. If you are asthmatic, then you know very well what it is to be starved of breath. If you are free of obvious breathing difficulties, then you probably take breathing for granted, but you can benefit greatly from expanding and exploring your capacity to breathe slowly and deeply. Conscious, rhythmic breathing is better for you than a cup of coffee, a sugar fix, or antidepressants of any kind. Some of the benefits established by scientific research include improved brain function, reduced blood lactate, improved immune function, reductions in bad cholesterol and increases in good cholesterol, and reduced blood pressure.

Our body, mind, and spirit compose a single and intraoperative system that amounts to human "being." The condition of each influences the others in a continuous feedback loop that builds on itself—whether for good or ill. Our breath is a means of intervention that can bring us back to balance and well-being. It is a point on the loop over which we have some measure of direct and immediate conscious control—more than we have over which hormones we release or our immune function, for example—so we can use the breath for self correction, self alignment, and self help. It is such a simple thing and yet so powerful. It is something that everyone can understand and practice.

In moments of stress, in moments when you recognize that you have been "lost in thought," you can raise your awareness and your performance by the simple act of breathing in a steady and rhythmic way.

The yoga practice of pranayama has been developed over thousands of years; adepts are capable of extraordinary feats of breath control. If you are a free diver, then you make it your business to learn how to hold your breath for more than six minutes in order to be able to dive to incredible depths. If you are a practicing lawyer, you do not need to operate at these extremes, yet you and your practice benefit if you bring your attention regularly to your breath.

The HeartMath method includes establishing a rhythmical respiration that brings the heart into coherence. As explained previously, this leads to entrainment of the autonomic nervous system, release of the highly beneficial hormone DHEA, and boosting of the immune system and cortical facilitation. Studies have shown that practicing the HeartMath methods delivers statistically significant improvements in quality of working and episodic memory and in cognitive reaction time.

I heartily recommend the Holosync suite of products from Centerpoint that use "binaural beat" to great effect. Binaural beat was re-discovered in the 1970s and became more accessible as portable cassette players became popular and affordable. The brain detects the difference between two frequencies (one in each ear) and "entrains" the predominant frequency of brain waves towards that difference. For example, alpha waves equate with a relaxed, receptive state and range between 7 and 13 hertz; our brain waves operate below about 40 hertz. Holosync has a direct impact on the autonomic nervous system and so has considerable physiological benefits. I notice that as soon as I use Holosync that if my nose is blocked on one side or both (other than when I have a head cold), it clears almost immediately, which is a sure sign to me that something is happening. It's like a spa treatment for my brain.

Very few lawyers will be immune to the effects on their physiological system, and therefore their psychological well-being, of the inherent stresses involved in legal practice. The simple fact is that we need to look after ourselves, body and mind and spirit, if we are to serve our clients' interests and our own to the best of our abilities.

It is in every lawyer's interest to take responsibility first for his or her well-being. Self-management has to take in the whole person: mind, body, spirit. Coping strategies are not what I am proposing. Such strategies involve leaving things as they are and learning how to adapt, or rather, maladapt, to them. If a situation does you harm, then it is not sustainable because you will not be sustainable—and without you, without your full capacity and attention, there will eventually be breakdown and failure for you and your practice.

Summary

- Self-management includes understanding and listening to your body that has innate intelligence

- The body is not just a vehicle but an integral part of our consciousness

- Mind and body influence each other and can enhance or degrade our conscious experience and capacities

- We should be aware and take notice of heart-felt and gut responses as these areas of our body have neurons and are an integral part of our intelligence

- We can work with our breathing to bring ourselves into a more relaxed and receptive state so that we can perform better and undo the harm caused by stress

- Visualization and positive self-talk are powerful means by which we can coach and support ourselves in order to be and do well for ourselves and others

- Neurogenesis, the creation of new neurons, is increased and supported by diet, exercise, sleep, and learning whereas stress and sleep deprivation, for example, are detrimental

- Lawyers are expected to perform to a high standard and operate in a competitive and adversarial environment and, like athletes, must look after their mental, physical and spiritual well-being if they are to sustain their careers

Integrity

The word *integrity* is most often used among lawyers when integrity is believed to be in question. Integrity used in this way means "the quality of being honest and having strong moral principles; moral uprightness" (*New Oxford Dictionary of English*). While integrity in this sense is, of course, important, I would like to explore integrity in the context of its other meaning: "the state of being whole and undivided."

Having touched on the essential integrity of body, mind, and spirit, I would now like to consider the integrity of meaning, purpose, and values that can be referred to as "authenticity." The experience of authenticity is also sometimes described as "being true to yourself." Truth is a tough one—the subject of much personal searching and philosophical enquiry. Psychologist and author Dr. David Fontana, in his book *The Meditator's Handbook*, says that "like Jung, I take the view that when we move into this kind of debate, the test of 'truth' is usefulness. Any concept which helps our inner growth is 'true' until we progress to a point were something more useful is needed."

Imagine making a solemn oath to yourself and others that "the life I live shall be one of truth, whole truth, and nothing but truth." How does that feel? Well, it feels extremely challenging to me and yet exhilarating when I think that it might be achievable. To live in such a way requires courage, particularly in the early stages of the transition and personal transformation that follow.

Finding your meaning and purpose is something that we hear and read about often these days. The language can suggest that finding meaning and purpose will have a specific and finite outcome: "So there they are. I have been looking for those everywhere. Done." I prefer and recommend the approach of finding meaning and purpose as an ongoing process that allows us to continuously journey, discover, and appreciate the differences in our experiences.

My sense is that our ultimate meaning lies in consciousness and our capacity to express ourselves through purpose. I see purpose as directed energy, a condition in which intention is formed internally and then takes external form through deliberate action. In his book Authentic Business, Neil Crofts has this to say about purpose:

> Having a profound purpose opens up the opportunity to be passionate about what you do, to be excited when you talk about it, to really care that it works and to engage, excite and inspire others with your message. Passion leads to creativity and commitment. If you are passionate about what you do you will have access to huge reserves of that creativity and commitment to overcome obstacles, to find solutions to problems and to persist. Without the passion, you might give up. Having and working with your profound purpose gives meaning to life and enables you to love what you do.

What shapes our purpose are our values. Our values are simply all those things that we believe are important; they need not be limited to the grander varieties of Superman's truth, justice, and the American way or the Greeks' cardinal virtues. Values change in nature and in importance as we ourselves change and grow. There are unquestionably patterns to our values and to the behaviours that flow from them. Systems such as Maslow's hierarchy, Beck and Cowan's Spiral Dynamics, and Richard Barrett's Seven Levels of Consciousness offer fascinating insights into our common, and to some degree, predictable humanity. Positive Psychology and the work of Martin Seligman point to the benefits and means of directing energy towards personal strengths and virtues. Values are at once profoundly personal and at the same time provide a channel for connection and cooperation with others.

Values are not good or bad, right or wrong, so long as they do not have as their purpose deliberate harm to others. Values are just what we find most important at a moment in time. When we live in accordance with our values, we are living according to what is true for us. When we do not, we are creating internal conflict that will inevitably manifest itself in external conflicts. Not being true to ourselves is inherently stressful. Honestly recognizing what we value most can be a testing and sometimes emotional process as we confront ourselves with what we truly seek and perhaps have lacked the courage to do.

For some people, pursuing authenticity involves a complete change of course. However, finding meaning and purpose does not necessarily involve drastic change. For most lawyers, it means rediscovering and reinvigorating our vocation. If you are fed up with legal practice, perhaps you are fed up with the way you have been practicing; you can begin addressing that by forming an intention to practice in a new way.

Looking afresh at what we value and the values we share in common with our colleagues can be all that is needed to lighten our step and illuminate the way ahead. In his book Liberating the Corporate Soul, Richard Barrett has this to say about the benefits of sharing common values: "Shared values build trust, and trust gives employees responsible freedom. Responsible freedom unlocks meaning and creativity. True power lies not in the ability to control but in the ability to trust."

The important thing to recognize about meaning and purpose, authenticity, mission, vision, values, and truth is that they are not about competition or differentiation; they are about what is true for you—what is useful for personal growth or for growth as an organization. Authenticity is not a contrived condition to be exploited for some material gain. Authenticity is a profoundly genuine and unique expression of you or your organization. There is no need to see what answers others have given to the question. It is not an exam in which you will be marked. Do not worry about being different. All you have to do is find your own words, your own way, your own truth; that will be distinctive and distinction enough.

WHAT IS YOUR LAW FIRM FOR?

This is a question that should be regularly addressed by partners, associates, and staff in every law firm, however small or large. Your first inclination may be to set about articulating the vision and objectives of the firm. This is, after all, a popular thing to do. To be truly worthwhile, however, the inquiry should be focused on establishing meaning and purpose that can be genuinely shared by everyone working within the firm and recognized by everyone outside the firm. Authenticity is a worthy and sustainable condition for any individual and any organization.

To establish mission, values, meaning, and purpose for a firm is to set a common reference point for the collective consciousness of everyone in the firm and for each person individually. The essential questions are: What do we belong to? Do I belong here? Challenging though it is, we have to "clean the windows" in order to be able to see clearly. If we don't, it is all too easy to become accustomed to living within a context that becomes steadily less in touch with what is going on outside, a "comfort zone" that steadily closes in and blocks vision.

There are various layers to this process that are distinct and yet can be integrated when undertaken consciously, just as when we decide what we value in our own personal "hierarchy of needs." These layers can and do exist concurrently; we need not surrender or deny one in preference to others. The common metaphor is that of peeling an onion, which evokes, in my mind at least, discomfort and some pain unless a lot of water is used on hands, blade, and the onion itself. Water is a symbol of emotion, and this process is one that can never be properly undertaken without regard to feelings and emotions.

A sense of balance in our lives, and particularly in the work that is part of our lives, is derived from the true sense of integration of our values with experience. The experiences of stress and distress are often based in a temporary loss of this integration. Peace, harmony, and integrity are our natural state just as has been shown to be the case with our physiology. It is when we depart from this natural coherence that we are placed under strain. If we are to have a happy life experience and a successful work experience, then we need to take care of ourselves and take care that our environment does not militate against our well-being.

Like dirty windows, stress is a condition to which we can gradually become maladapted; stress closes us in, obscuring our view of things as they truly are. I once persuaded myself that stress was something I thrived on when others couldn't. Where pressures did not exist, I was sure to create them for myself and consequently for others. Running on the treadmill and increasing the pace so preoccupied my attention that I did not make time for stillness, for exploring and listening to myself. The solution, in the end, was to pull the plug. While I worked hard to serve clients and create future stability and success for members of my firm, I spent almost no time with my family, which I deeply regret, and even less with myself.

Of course, nothing is so black and white. I loved what I was doing; leading a fast-growing business created opportunities for many good people. My own values in leading that business were simple and repeatedly expressed. However, as time went on and as the business grew, I saw how those values were being eroded. I did not have the personal strength to reverse the trend. In the early years, I used my pruning shears wherever needed, and as a result the firm grew strong and flourished. As time went on, I persuaded myself that I should be more tolerant, that the firm was now broad enough in the beam to carry those who preferred to sit on the side of more traditional behaviour.

In the early 1990s, while taking a route through one of the office buildings in Central Hong Kong to avoid either heat or rain, I came across the book Leadership Is an Art by Max De Pree. I left the shop without it, but something within me told me to go back and buy it. I am so glad I did. There is so much wisdom and many important lessons to be found in this book. The one I remember most is the one that I tried my hardest to convey to my former partners—namely, the proposition that as leaders we make a covenant with those whom we invite to work in our business to do our utmost to create conditions in which they can express their unique humanity.

A law firm can provide everyone within the firm, regardless of their place in the hierarchy of authority, with an equal opportunity to grow into their potential and realize their aspirations, so long as doing so respects the needs of the firm and the greater good of its members. I found nothing more rewarding than seeing people in my firm achieving what they so often believed was beyond their reach. I saw people at all levels having fun and did my utmost to create the conditions in which it was possible to do so. My achievements in building my firm might be measured from the outside by reference to turnover, offices, and other measures of power. However, what mattered then and what matters most now is the satisfaction of seeing others find fulfilment through their work in the firm.

The cynical reader may find this all a little too mushy. After all, isn't it all in the end about money and power? Does anybody really care? Is there really any alternative to the school of hard knocks? If that is what you think, then that is what you will continue to reproduce in your own life and in the lives of the unfortunate people who work with you. Cynicism is to values as sarcasm is to wit: a poor and bitter substitute. What science can now show, and what has been known across centuries, no doubt, is that stress undermines performance and causes lasting harm.

We have so faithfully learned the way that we were taught that we perpetuate a command and control culture that is fundamentally flawed and unsuitable in our modern context. We have to be willing to look at things differently if we are to face these challenges. A problem cannot be solved with the same type of consciousness that created it, as Einstein is often credited with explaining.

MACHINE OR ORGANISM?

Oscar Ichazo, philosopher and founder of Psychocalisthenics, has these observations to make regarding our attitude to the human body, which seem to me to be equally applicable to the body of an organization:

> We make of our body a gross material image that, as a machine, has to puff, sweat, get overheated and exhausted—all as a part of a high-performance. Our problem is that we are not a machine but an organism, and that simple analogies between them are destined to miss the point. As a living organism our body is an integrity and its optimum functioning can only be measured not in terms of performance, like a machine, but in terms of health as an organism.

How do we understand health, then? Aaron Antonovsky, in his 1987 paper entitled "Unraveling the Mystery of Health: How People Manage Stress and Stay Well," explains it as follows:

> We are coming to understand health not as the absence of disease, but as the process by which individuals maintain their sense of coherence (i.e. sense that life is comprehensible, manageable and meaningful) and ability to function in the face of changes in themselves and their relationships with their environment.

Like most things, the law, taken at a single moment in time, is apparently fixed and unchanging; however, it is in fact constantly changing, like everything else in reality—change is not an option. It is sometimes said in higher education that the pace of change is such that what is learned, in the field of technology and science, at least, will remain valid for little more than 18 months. Legal practice also faces increasing complexity and pace of change in law, regulation, professional obligations, risks, and relationships. In addition to dealing with changes in the law, lawyers are also expected to assimilate new information and communications technologies—and the expectations those give rise to—inside and outside the firm.

What is rigid and fixed may seem strong, but in the end it is only hard and brittle. The kind of strength that is needed in the face of changing demands and conditions is rooted in flexibility. In the command and control mindset, creating fixed procedures, pipelines, and processes is the surest way to predictable outcome and profit. When everything moved at a slower pace, such an approach worked for the legal profession as much as it did for industry. There was time for supervision of one kind or another.

Supervision requires time if it is to be used as an opportunity for training and mentoring. In the frenetic pace of today's legal practice, there is precious little time given to such supervision because lawyers at all levels—in particular, partners—rush to fill their timesheets with six minutes' worth of time charged (to parody a line from Rudyard Kipling's "If"). A considerable degree of self-organization is implicitly expected and practically necessary.

Rather than recognizing and supporting this self-organization, many firms provide a long leash, which is then yanked on from time to time or used to throttle the individual when blame needs to be apportioned. It is a culture of blame and fear that predominates in legal practice today. Though most lawyers somehow adapt to these conditions and the stress they cause, this culture is one of the root causes of the public's low regard for lawyers.

The law firm is an organism of sorts. It is primarily organic, in the sense that it is made up of a collection of human beings who consent to work together and whose collective energies can be directed towards excellence and success or dissipated towards mediocrity and failure. Just as the human body responds to fear and stress, so does the collective body of a firm. If you regard your firm as a moneymaking business, a machine that generates wealth for its owners, then you can expect to create your firm in that image. For some, that is enough. If, however, you regard your firm as a living and evolving organism, then you can allow that organism to create itself and grow by drawing on a form of energy far more powerful than money.

I do not believe that lawyers want to work primarily for money any more than any other person does. Even putting aside the notion of vocation, surely our shared ideal is to do what we love and get paid well for doing it. A sure sign that we are not well in ourselves and in our work is when our focus is solely on our salary or profit share. If we feel exploited, then there is an issue that must be addressed immediately for the benefit of the individual and the firm as a whole. If we feel motivated, we are by definition clear about our motive, our reason for moving forward, and this benefits us individually and the firm as a whole.

Shared values, shared direction, shared motivation—these are what makes a firm more than the sum of its parts.

The purpose in all this is to get to the heart of what makes a healthy firm and what undermines that health. Both inside and outside the profession, we speak about good firms and bad firms, just as we do about country firms, city firms, and international firms. Whether or not a firm is considered "good to work for" is the stuff of rumour and gossip, which usually emphasizes the negative. Whether a firm is good to and for its members is evidenced by such indicators as levels of sickness and absence, staff turnover, partner departures, and so on. Being an "employer of choice" means more than packages and perks.

Each firm must decipher itself, getting to the heart of its meaning and purpose to identify what can be shared explicitly by every member of the firm for no less important reason than to engage and direct their energies. A firm that knows itself, that recognizes and nurtures integrity, is one that "walks the talk" and displays a confidence and ease that is as attractive to clients as it is to new talent.

You may well be thinking that this sort of talk is all very well, but "we have a business to run." This is, of course, true; the business has particular needs distinct from those of the individual. Yet those needs can be conceptually and practically aligned with the needs of the individual; this is a subject I explore in some detail in Chapter 6. The business demands a certain discipline and order, particularly in the area of billing and collections. This is an area in which law firms are traditionally weak and lawyers traditionally indifferent. When, however, everyone in the business understands the essential principles and dynamics at work, it is possible to operate a professional services business in a way that does not deviate from stated values.

The Mars Corporation, one of the largest privately owned organizations in the world, operates by referring to what are known as the five principles. These principles are regularly discussed by everyone in the organization at every level, providing guidance for attitude, direction, and conduct. The principles are quality, responsibility, mutuality, freedom, and efficiency. The freedom principle is one that is of particular importance to the reluctance that many lawyers feel with regard to charging and recovering fees. Though non-lawyers might laugh at the idea, most lawyers do struggle when it comes to fees. What the Mars website has to say about freedom is this:

> Mars history shows that freedom can be achieved in another way and profit is the key. Profit allows us to remain free, to invest wisely, to ensure short-term lows in return for long-term highs, and to run the business in our own distinctive man-

ner. Freedom as a company means freedom for individuals to find better ways to reach our common goals.

I had the privilege of serving Mars as a client and have had firsthand experience of the enormous power and energy of this global organization, managed as it was then by some 35 people working from a small office in Washington State. I do not believe that these five principles are idle ideals gathering dust or conjured up as part of a modern fad for "mission and value statements." They are principles articulated by the founders of the business and, I suspect, are as relevant to the success of the business today as they ever were.

What is important here is that whatever values are articulated, they have to be used, and noticed being used, if they are not to be dulled by cynicism and honoured only in the breach. Values are in some way a little like clothing; although many of us wear the same clothes, we all manage to wear them slightly differently. One only has to think of the ways children wear school uniforms to recognize the huge scope for individual expression. Think about how we uniquely express ourselves and the values in which we clothe our actions. Values without our active expression of them are never more than attractive concepts.

DEFENDING VALUES

Consider our personal lives. Some elements we judge as beneficial and rewarding. At the same time, other elements we consider irritating, depressing, or simply bland and mundane. Most of us choose to suppress or deny the areas that are not so bright, not doing so well, and concentrate instead on the good things. Many times, this is the right way to carry on until such time as one of those more difficult areas becomes so difficult that it can no longer be ignored.

In the context of a business, it is quite common for us to similarly compartmentalize and accept that there are parts of the business, or more likely people working in parts of the business, who are not behaving in a way that is conducive to harmony and progress for the business. Here lies great danger. Failure to address such areas of the business and those people who are not operating in accordance with the values that have been established is to store up trouble in the present that will lead to conflict in the future.

The corporate or professional body, like the physical body, needs to be well balanced in all areas to avoid building up tension and resistance that will ultimately bring about acute pain or failure. By recognizing and dealing with these difficult areas while they are still relatively dormant, we can address them in a way that is conducive to a solution rather than to conflict. I speak of this from my own experience, having allowed a situation to arise in my own professional business that over time became so entrenched that I could no longer see a way to reverse it. The situation that developed became such that I no longer felt at home in my own firm.

It is easy to hold values dear and yet allow them to be undermined by what begins as the smallest behavioural anomalies and ultimately becomes something that takes on its own destructive power. Each one of us can, in one moment, pay lip service to a principle or value and, in the next, act in clear contravention of that principle without finding any cause for concern or justification for change. In order to honour the values that are essential to our emotional and spiritual well-being, we must be vigilant for what is incongruous and what works against those values. To do this requires active awareness; it requires conscious thought and conscious behaviour.

What I am proposing here is not easy. It demands great discipline and compassion. I am not advocating that you ruthlessly excise anything that may be seen as bad or unsuited to the business. I am saying that we should be aware of it, learn from it, and deal with it in a timely and proportional manner.

Summary

- Integrity of meaning, purpose and values underpins authenticity

- A sense of purpose arises from what we value and so allows us to direct our energy to what we consider to be good purpose

- Our values change or evolve as we progress through life and just as we free to choose what is true for us we may find and pursue new priorities

- When we live in accordance with our values, we are living according to what is true for us, and when we do not we create internal conflict

- Lawyers can refresh their sense of meaning and purpose by rediscovering and reinvigorating their vocation to serve others who need legal advice and representation

- Values, when clearly articulated and genuinely shared, promote trust among members of an organization

- Organizations and their leaders can provide the frame within which individuals pursue their meaning and purpose to drive and sustain growth and profitability for their good and that of the organization

- Rather than being machines, professional firms are better regarded and treated as organisms that flex and evolve from within to deal with changing conditions and demands

- Stated values must be seen to be lived out in an organization if their importance is not to be diminished by cynicism

- Defending values requires discipline and compassion in addressing behaviours that undermine them

Alignment and Coherence

Professional business has come a long way since I first joined the legal profession in 1979, at least at a superficial level. Whereas once it was considered almost indecent to promote one's services, today's professional businesses employ a broad range of marketing techniques. It is now common—indeed, expected—that a professional business will set out not just the services that it is able to provide but also some form of mission statement, vision, and values. Firms and professional groups within large corporate organizations have embraced the notion of creating a brand, and many are now expected to engage actively with clients and the wider market through social media.

In the context of marketing of consumer products, the brand has been described as "one think shopping," the simple trust-choice that every business would like its customers to make. Consumer products must live up to customer expectations, which can to some degree be managed by after-sales service. In professional services, the product is one of daily interaction, and performance is ultimately judged by the client's service experience and not just by the outcome of an individual project.

One of the most commonly stated values in professional business these days is "our people are our most important asset." These and other obviously noble values, once stated, can easily be devalued by the cynicism that follows when those values are not lived up to. Whereas aspirations are by definition yet to be attained, it is expected that values are observed and therefore that they align with actual experience. Achieving such alignment is a considerable challenge and involves striking a balance among the interests of the individual lawyer, the individual owner (of the firm), the organization, the client, and all others with whom the business interacts.

The importance of alignment goes far deeper than simply being observed doing what is right or what you promised to do. It is the means by which the individual and the collective (the people in your firm) generate, release, and share energy. By *energy* I mean such qualities as willingness, readiness, enthusiasm, motivation, creativity, and innovation. The importance of these energetic qualities is easily understood; simply imagine where you or your business would be without any one of them. The complete absence of energy is rare; more commonly, it is simply in short supply.

Consider the four essential elements of a firm (intellectual, emotional, functional, and financial). None is relevant without the others. However, the intellectual and emotional elements are dominant and entirely human factors, not susceptible to the same measurement and control as the other two. However business-like a firm might try to be, it is never going to be other than a voluntary collective of individuals engaging in professional service.

While it may be an attractive idea to some to have everyone perform exactly the same and precisely according to plan, humans stubbornly resist becoming carbon copies of each other. Recognizing the benefits of diversity and idiosyncrasy is about accepting and working with the way we are rather than fighting it in the name of certainty and control. As Immanuel Kant put it in his *Idea for a General History from a Cosmopolitan Perspective*: "Out of the crooked timber of humanity no straight thing was ever made."

People can and do work together, and become more than the sum of their parts, precisely because they are different. A firm is not a construct of plastic people snapped together into a money-making machine. It is a constantly evolving organic form capable of incredible achievement or stultifying mediocrity. There is so much room for creativity and personality in legal service, yet it is often suppressed by fear-driven management styles.

When it is present, alignment gives rise to a condition that I will call *coherence*. A common dictionary definition of the term is "the quality of being logically integrated, consistent, and intelligible," as in a coherent argument. Thoughts and emotional states can be coherent (which is positive) or incoherent (which is negative). The thoughts and emotional states of the people in a firm determine the intellectual and emotional conditions in the firm. Coherence in a professional organization can only be achieved through a predominance of coherence among the individuals that make up the firm.

Achieving coherence and "flow" is something that can be learned and consciously practiced once you have a basic understanding of the human condition and how to make the best of it. That understanding is the springboard to a deeper recognition of the interdependencies that exist in a firm, what the consequences are of imbalances and negative behaviours on health and performance, and what can be done to address them.

ALIGNING INDIVIDUAL AND BUSINESS NEEDS

While we talk about "the firm" and recognize it as an intellectual concept, we generally do not look closely at the specific needs of the business. One way to do this is to consider the needs of individuals and of the business in order to identify a language of alignment. *Alignment* is another way of saying that things fit together. Alignment denotes congruence, coherence, and matching points of contact or lines of sight.

When working as a coach with some businesses, I like to include an empty chair at the meeting table to denote the notional place of the business. The business cannot observe or contribute other than through the medium of those present; it is unrepresented until one or more becomes its advocate and protector. A business may at times need to be protected from its owners and owners do well to distinguish their own needs from those of the business. The business has a life of sorts that is in the hands of the owners, and there is an essential interdependence that can and should be respected.

I will now look at a selection of six elements that comprise a firm, matching corresponding aspects of the individual, the business, and performance measures. These are set out in the table below. In the central column are suggested words intended to reflect shared interest and alignment. It is important to bear in mind that while one can find a common language of alignment, doing so does not make the interests and values of the participants the same and need not do so. The key with alignment is to inquire deeply into the values and interests of every participant and remember that each remains essentially different. Differences do not preclude alignment so long as there is enough common ground for genuine coherence.

Rather than looking at alignment between, for example, associates and partners, I have used the firm itself. This is because it is important to see the firm as a participant in the whole with its own particular needs and interests. Notice the pervading themes of relationship, of perception and experience, and of interdependence.

Business	Measure	**Alignment**	Measure	Individual
Resources	Utilization	**Synchrony**	Flow	Energy
Function	Reliability	**Loyalty**	Dedication	Application
Interaction	Cooperation	**Harmony**	Ease	Relating
Information	Capture/Retrieval	**Knowledge**	Discernment	Experience
Operations	Accuracy	**Quality**	Adeptness	Skills
Revenues	Profitability	**Reward**	Commensurate	Income

Try substituting words and concepts of your own as a means of testing your own ideas and finding out how others see things.

RESOURCES/ENERGY

Resources in a business refer to the latent capacities and capabilities that exist at any one time. They can be used, unused, overused, and underused. We identify what each and every resource is and then determine what level of utilization is being achieved and the efficiency with which those resources are used together. A primary factor in determining the successful functioning of a business is that resources are directed precisely when and where they are needed.

The resources of an individual similarly refer to our capacities and capabilities. Rather than focusing on utilization, our internal measure of the successful operation of our consciousness is one of flow. Flow suggests ease and harmony and, at the same time, fulfilment. When our energy is flowing, it is released consistently and continuously to good purpose without leaving us stressed or drained.

Alignment of the needs of the business and the individual therefore revolve around the idea of synchrony; in other words, everything is done as, when, and where it should be. The ideal is therefore harnessing each individual's flow of energy as part of the efficient utilization of the firm's resources.

It is perhaps easier to think of examples of where synchrony does not exist: where we see friction, lack of cooperation, people "running around like headless chickens" (not a pleasant image). Synchrony can be seen when everyone is working together with confidence and ease and tasks are getting done as and when they should. Energy is not dissipated in needless friction. It is something you can sense rather than measure in terms of time and money. That said, it is my experience that when you get it right, the money comes.

FUNCTION/APPLICATION

When it comes to the people in the business, the business wants those people to perform their individual functions properly and reliably. Reliability is a vital aspect of functionality because without it the business cannot predict performance. The business thrives on predictable outcomes and has no interest in being anything other than what it is. A business can only innovate and grow if it is not held back by inconsistency in essential functional performance.

The equivalent of function in the individual is application. An individual is capable of being present yet not applying himself to his expected functions in the business. This is sometimes referred to as *presenteeism*. The individual is "in the building" but not doing what is expected of him; the loss of function may not be as immediately apparent to the business as absence would make it.

When an individual applies himself fully to serving the interests of the business, we can describe this as dedication. Dedication is a wholehearted application of capacities and capabilities to the purposes of the business. What the business is looking for, and what the individual is asked to give, is a consistency that amounts to loyalty.

INTERACTION/RELATING

A business looks for the productive interaction of its resources and the most important of these interactions are those among the people in the business. The business looks to its people to cooperate efficiently—in other words, to operate collectively and coherently so as to achieve optimal utilization. Whereas for an individual the term *cooperation* is charged with an emotional element that is positive, cooperation from the point of view of the business is emotionally neutral. The business wants its people and other resources to operate together to perform their respective functions in the most efficient and effective manner possible.

The comparable facet for the individual is relating. In the case of the individual, interactions with others are for the purpose of relating. This activity of relating literally tells, or relates, the story of the individual's identity in the context of the business and the stories that the individual constructs about others in the business (the relationships). This relating is a fundamentally emotional activity played out in the context of the business and its hierarchy of power. For the individual, the measure of successful relating is one of ease. Where there is cooperation in interactions and ease in relationships, there can be said to be harmony.

INFORMATION/EXPERIENCE

While the business cannot acquire experience, it can record information, which can then be used by individuals to substantiate and reinforce experience. The business has no capacity for independent differentiation or thought, so it cannot form experience without the benefit of intelligence. An individual has real intelligence, which can be applied to information so that the individual can apply judgment.

The business can support the individual in performing her unique function. It can capture information created inside and outside the business and provide means of retrieval. The business can also provide the conditions within which knowledge can be exchanged between people inside and outside the business in the course of their interactions. The point of convergence for the interests of the business and the individual lies in the field of what is commonly referred to as knowledge.

OPERATIONS/SKILLS

Putting to one side the emotional component of the lawyer-client relationship, the measure of success from the perspective of the business is accuracy. For the business to continue as a professional practice, professional activities should be conducted without error or omission. Although service quality amounts to more than purely professional accuracy, without it, business risks increase, causing uncertainty, instability, and possibly failure.

The individual's equivalent of professional and accurate operations is her application of professional skills. The measure for the individual is whether she is adept in those skills. The alignment between business and individual lies in the area of quality.

REVENUES/INCOME

Revenues, in the form of professional fees, are the oxygen carried in the lifeblood of a firm. As the resources of the firm are expended in providing service, so they must be replenished if the firm is to continue to provide that service. If the flow of revenues is constricted or diverted, then the firm cannot continue to provide service at the same level—or perhaps at all.

Generating fees is not a necessary evil that complicates or interferes with the provision of services. Billing and collection are not unpleasant activities that detract from the lawyer–client relationship. Fees are oxygen, and the body of the firm cannot survive or thrive without breathing in and breathing out. Fees are a mark of value exchanged and an integral part of the service relationship. To ignore or to be in any way embarrassed by the subject of fees is foolish and dangerous for both the business and for the client relationship.

A healthy business not only produces sufficient revenues to meet its outgoings but also generates profit with which to invest. In a legal practice dedicated to continuity and growth, profits will be invested in training, research, marketing, recruitment, and relationships. In practices concerned with maximizing returns to the current partners, profits will invariably be distributed immediately to those partners, with no investment in the business or its people.

For the individual, the key issue is being valued in a way that is commensurate with his or her position, responsibilities, and contributions, taken in the context of the overall "market" and rewards obtained by peers. In just about all firms, incomes are kept secret, whereas revenues and costs of the business may be made public within the firm. If incomes are kept secret, then it is possible to deal with each individual and that individual's perception of their worth to the business within the parameters of market rates. In my view, a reward system must either be completely transparent or completely opaque; there is really no in-between ground.

For the business and for the individual—whether associate or partner or staff—the common denominator is reward. The business has no emotional attachment or participation in reward, but for the individual the emotional element, and the associated perception of self-worth, is paramount.

MARKETING

Marketing is an activity that, quite honestly, makes most lawyers uncomfortable. There are many reasons for this, the greatest of which is the simple human anxiety regarding rejection. We all want to be liked, appreciated, respected, and valued. We believe we are worthy of the opportunity to provide service to clients—and yet at the same time, we plainly don't.

Marketing is an activity, but it is first and foremost an attitude. It begins and succeeds through attitude and is undermined by doubt. Marketing is telling your story in order to sell. Discussions around marketing tend to focus on specific techniques or tactics employed by others, but we often need to first challenge our fear of rejection and unwillingness to present ourselves as wanting more work.

Essentially, marketing involves no more than telling people what you do and that you would like to do more of it—if possible, for them. If you really wanted to let people know how much you enjoy your work, how much you enjoy serving client interests, how confident you are in the capabilities of your colleagues and your firm, then what on earth could prevent you from conveying that to anyone who will listen? Just as with most things, we can think of a thousand reasons for not doing something, yet we require only one reason to do it. Find that reason and you will have no difficulty in finding your best way of communicating and marketing.

One of the simplest techniques is to make your existing clients aware that you would like more work, not only from them but also from others to whom they may be willing to recommend your firm's services. If you tell your clients that you are busy, then they will simply assume that you do not have the capacity for more. If you do not tell them anything, then they likely again will assume that you do not wish for more work. If you do not blow your own trumpet, no one else is going to blow it for you.

More work will seldom be thrust upon you, or, if it is, then it is unlikely to be the kind of work that you would really like to be doing. If you tell your clients that you would like more work, or tell clients that you or your firm have other skills that could be employed by the client, then, without placing any personal pressure on the client, you may find the client surprised and pleased to hear of your additional capacity.

I remember an occasion involving a major client of my firm for whom we had handled a substantial anti-counterfeiting matter in the UK. Over a lunch meeting, the client mentioned some ongoing litigation involving trade libel.

My immediate thought, of course, was why the client had not thought of us when it came to choosing their lawyers in that action. Through gentle probing, I discovered that the client simply did not know that we could handle that kind of work.

I realized then that though we had an excellent relationship with the client, and though the client held my colleagues in the highest regard, they had clearly put the firm into a particular service category, and we had missed the opportunity to tell them of our interest in providing services in other fields. This, of course, has to be done gently and not so as to give rise to any sense of obligation on the part of the client to bring you work just because you have established a new department or hired new skills into the firm that allow you to provide that service.

Similarly, a former editor of the *Legal 500* told me a story of a meeting with a major corporate client of a large city firm. He asked the in-house counsel what he thought of the new approach that the firm in question had been taking with regard to crossover skills between two of their departments which included services to that client. The client said he had no views because he simply didn't know anything about it. Either the firm had failed to pass on their change in practices to their client or, perhaps more likely, the client had simply not understood how the information was relevant to him and to his organization.

Marketing activities such as writing articles, speaking at conferences, and holding internal seminars are tried and tested means of engaging with existing and potential clients; content marketing, webcasting, and meetups are new manifestations of well-trodden paths, and I do not propose to examine them here. Attention spans have become ever shorter so, while business social media is the new black, I believe there is still real relationship value in methods that might be regarded as old-fashioned, such as time spent over a meal together. (Time for a "slow marketing" movement, perhaps?)

What is important to emphasize is the fact that marketing is a day-to-day, moment-to-moment expression of the brand and values of a firm. Marketing includes every interaction you have with everyone that is in any way involved with your firm. Marketing is not a big smile to an audience; it is the sincere and considerate dealing with others much in the way that you would like to be dealt with yourself. Your dealings with suppliers, other firms, and everyone you contact in the course of your business are marketing activities. Whenever you are engaging with anyone outside yourself you are conveying essential messages about the character, personality, and style of your business.

Marketing is not an activity that should be reserved only for partners or associates in a firm. Every member of staff, especially support staff, has a huge role to play in marketing the business of the firm. We all know how important our administrative assistants are to us and how we value their opinions of the behaviours of others. Just think how important it is
for your client's PA to give a good report of interactions with people in your firm.

The kind of marketing that I am talking about is quite different from the kind designed to demonstrate how powerful and clever you are. The kind of marketing that I am talking about demonstrates only what is true about you and the values that you bring to bear in the conduct of your practice.

WORKSPACE AND OFFICE ARCHITECTURE

Law firms tend to follow a very traditional office layout. Reception and client meeting rooms are kept apart and usually out of view of lawyers and staff at work. The format is essentially the same as for a dentist or doctor's surgery; the client waits in a holding area and is given something to read before being ushered into a "treatment" room. These rooms are generally well furnished and well appointed, with a nice view, coffee, and old books.

When it comes to the working areas the common principles are these:

- Lawyers have rooms with windows. The size of these rooms and views they enjoy usually depend on seniority (the "corner office" standard).
- Partners generally have rooms to themselves. Associates often share. Paralegals and unqualified fee earners may be grouped together or work in open space alongside secretaries.
- Secretaries and other support staff are usually placed within shouting distance, close to the door to the office or offices of those they work for. More often than not, secretaries and other support staff have little access to natural light from their workstations.
- Photocopying, print room, delivery, and other staff are generally in the basements and other areas no one else wishes to work in.

For those working in older buildings, this traditional format is encouraged by the layout of the space itself. What has tended to happen, however, in modern office buildings with an open layout is that the traditional format has been faithfully reproduced. The more flexible and open plan workstation approach found in other sectors and organizations has been successfully resisted. It strikes me that this resistance is just another manifestation of the general resistance to adapting to modern ways and forms of collaboration.

I had the opportunity to implement some simple ideas in the London office of my former firm based in Docklands, close to Canary Wharf. Here are some of the particular features that I believe worked well. The space was an open rectangular layout (11,000 square feet) with windows running the full length of the two long sides; there were also windows along half of one of the shorter sides and a third of the other.

- All lawyers and as many others as we could manage were placed close to windows. The lawyers' rooms always sat two people. Partners and senior lawyers were placed with trainees or junior associates so that there was maximum opportunity for learning.
- The internal partitions were glass so that natural light was not blocked in any way to the internal areas of the office.
- Only accounts and HR offices had doors. Doors are expensive and should be open anyway—if a private conversation was required, the meeting rooms with doors could be used.
- Low-level filing cabinets with natural wooden tops were used as dividers for secretarial workstations, allowing some privacy and protection but also permitting sightlines across the office from a seated position.
- The library was in a central position without division, offering equal access to all and a constant reminder that it existed.

Every space varies, and we have to make the best of what is available. It is important, however, to ask some fundamental questions of any layout or floor plan:

- Is this a fair use of the space we have?
- Does this layout give everyone as much access to natural light as possible?
- Does this layout serve to encourage collaborative working or discourage it?
- What does this layout say about us as a firm, internally and -externally?
- Does this layout express and reflect our values?

Lawyers stuck behind their desks, hiding things in drawers, closing doors—this is the traditional picture and the common reality. One study revealed that lawyers' offices are empty 60 percent of the time; we incur considerable costs maintaining something that is traditionally expected and yet not necessarily beneficial.

Measuring the economic benefits obtained by adopting new layouts and workspace use is only going to be possible once the investment has already been made. Frankly, my view has always been that "if you get it right, the money comes." An investment in creating genuinely better working conditions for everyone, not just the lawyers, will pay dividends in one form or another. Workspace is a vital element, dynamic in any firm, that deserves attention. You do not need to be a master of feng shui to figure out what works.

Summary

- It is expected that an organization's stated values are observed and align with actual experience

- Alignment entails striking a balance between the interests and expectations of all and, critically, between the individual and the organization

- When achieved, alignment gives rise to coherence among individuals so that their energy flows freely in service of the organization

- By examining essential capacities and interests of the business alongside those of individuals and how each is measured, one can arrive at a language of alignment

- Considering these matters brings about enquiry that serves to deepen understanding of the business and the individual, and their interdependence

- Understanding interdependencies and finding a language of alignment throws light on what individuals can do to serve the business and how in turn the business will be strengthened to better serve individual interests

- Conscious alignment between business and individual has a direct impact on winning new clients and work as everyone is clear and collective energy is unrestricted and well-directed

- Winning new clients and new work is vital to growth and so everyone, including support staff, has a role to play in marketing

- The most important form of marketing is that which is experienced by clients and others through daily interactions with members of your organization

- Consideration should be given to workspace and office architecture to ensure that working conditions are fair for all and aligned with stated values and culture

- An investment in creating genuinely better working conditions for everyone, not just the lawyers, will pay dividends when it comes to productive working relationships

Valuing Others

If you can learn to value yourself, then you can begin to value others. If you can allow yourself the opportunity to pursue authenticity, then you can encourage others to do so. Whereas judgment of others closes down relationship, valuing others opens up relationship. You will find that every relationship matters if you look for the value that every relationship holds for you and the value that you can contribute to it.

We take too many relationships for granted and persuade ourselves that we are too busy to give them our full attention even for a moment. In doing so we are not only missing out, we are also missing the point: Every Relationship Matters.

APPRECIATION AND REASSURANCE

There are few things quite so pleasing to receive as sincere appreciation. Money can buy appreciation of sorts but not the kind that really matters to us as human beings, the kind that is sincere and freely offered.

Appreciation lifts the spirits. It makes us feel valued and recognizes the contribution we have made to the other's benefit. Appreciation brings out the best in people and yet it is so seldom given, especially in professional service environments where "being busy" is invariably a self-aggrandizing behaviour that promotes melodrama rather than flow.

As many have said, "It doesn't cost anything to say thank you," and appreciation can be expressed in so many more ways, as well. Appreciation is experienced as genuine and meaningful when it demonstrates the recognition of our specific contribution. General blandishments do not constitute sincere appreciation. ("You're doing a great job" is one of the most common and patronizing examples.)

Showing appreciation is now commonly referred to as "feedback": positive feedback and constructive negative feedback. The purpose of both forms is to communicate something meaningful to the receiver in such a way that the receiver leaves with some reinforcement or learning. Handled correctly, feedback is a form of appreciation for the effort that has been made whether or not the outcome was as good as it might have been. Feedback is also one of the elements of "flow" experience.

It is important when showing appreciation to take the time to connect with the person you are speaking to—for example, by making eye contact—showing that you are truly interested. The time you give to appreciation is a measure of the success of the message and the benefit to the receiver. It is not possible to devalue the currency of appreciation other than through insincerity or poor delivery. The investment you make in showing appreciation pays dividends in so many ways.

If you are not someone who regularly shows appreciation, then perhaps it is time for you to take stock of how much you have to be grateful for from your colleagues, clients, friends, and family. You might start by showing appreciation towards yourself for the efforts and contributions that you have made; you might then feel more inclined and find it easier to show appreciation for others.

Reassurance is another important and underused practice that can serve to revitalize and inspire. Rather than always waiting for specific achievements or events to offer appreciation or feedback, we can offer words of reassurance that have the power to rekindle enthusiasm, restore commitment, and establish loyalty.

It is seldom that lawyers receive much in the way of thanks from clients, at least once the final bill has been delivered. Similarly, very few lawyers express their thanks to clients for the opportunity to provide service, to learn about them and their business, and to represent their interests. If you don't feel it, then don't say it. If, on the other hand, you are able to recognize and be genuinely grateful for the investment of trust and confidence—and not just fees—then you may find that expressing appreciation is the most natural thing to do.

As lawyers, we are arguably only doing what is expected of us and what any other lawyer with the equivalent training and experience should be able to achieve. Competence should be a given, and we are rightly expected to do what we are paid to do. That does not mean, however, that we do not crave and value sincere appreciation and reassurance. Knowing this about ourselves leads to the obvious conclusion that we should never miss an opportunity to extend it to others.

BEING VALUED

The sense of being valued is one fundamental to the human condition. It is at the core of our social conditioning and our desire to belong to the communities in which we take part. This is so obvious to all of us, yet its influence on our behaviour goes largely unrecognised. In the context of working life, and of a legal career, our sense of being valued has a direct impact on our behaviour and the conduct of our practice; status and income are key factors in this area.

In legal professional practice, there are commonly a number of tiers: partners, associates and other non-partners, professional support staff, and general support staff. Hierarchy is established around seniority in terms of legal qualification, years in practice, and partnership and reinforced through a corresponding hierarchy of reward. This hierarchy of reward is the primary measure of value to the firm and therefore the individual's sense of being valued.

Below partner level, salaries are generally kept secret, although just about anyone who puts his mind to it can find out what others are getting paid. The real concern that most have is whether they are paid less than their peers. The more objective the criteria for setting salary levels and the greater the transparency, the less it is likely that individuals will feel undervalued. To achieve this, however, requires recognition also of contributions made through non-fee earning work, something that cannot be achieved until non-chargeable time is recorded, managed, and valued with the same interest as chargeable time.

The major status hurdle for any lawyer is accession to partnership. Having achieved qualification, the years ahead represent a struggle to claw a way up the ladder to partnership. Very few have any idea what partnership will entail, or, for that matter, that in many larger firms it means little other than a title and increased income. The anxiety about, uncertainty regarding, and mystery surrounding partnership can be paralysing. Normal considerations for others can go out of the window in the months leading to possible accession as the great game is played out.

With the advent of alternative business structures for law firms in the UK, a development that is gradually having influence far beyond UK borders, there is now the added complexity of status, ownership, and reward within a corporate framework. That said, the names on the rungs of the ladder may change and the number of rungs may increase, but the objective for many is still to climb as high as possible.

The struggle for recognition, whether in terms of status or salary or both, leads to many placing themselves under a constant state of siege with regard to their self-worth and their value to the business. Little or no recognition is given for non-chargeable time or for time invested in supporting colleagues whether through formal or informal teaching, coaching, or mentoring. The clear message delivered in most firms is that it is client acquisition and billing that counts. Whether this is stated or implicit, most look to the examples set by high-earning partners who are held in awe and authority by the partnership and so by everyone within the firm. Demonstrating what you can bring to the firm in financial terms is what counts. Ordinary human needs to be trusted and valued are suppressed and anaesthetized by hard, long hours and perhaps a drink or three after work.

Modern thinkers concerned with the criteria for success in the knowledge era use another language. They do not speak of human resources, assets, and knowledge workers. They recognize the unique contribution of individuals and the responsibility of leadership to create an environment in which those individuals may flourish. They recognize the competitive advantage that can be gained by drawing out those human factors that go beyond process and time sheets. They look to qualities of creativity, insight, innovation, relationship building, and collaboration.

It is simple enough to understand that people are at their best when they feel valued. The opportunity is to identify all those contributions that are valuable and to recognize and reward them in financial and other ways.

EQUAL CONTRIBUTION

Hierarchy of responsibility gives rise to hierarchy of reward, and in most organizations this is acceptable if only because it has so long been the way of things. I have read of radical organizations in which management roles are appointed by the vote of all workers and whose remuneration is also fixed according to what is considered fair by the workforce. It's hard to imagine such a thing in a legal practice; however, we are living in a time when what seemed impossible is no longer so and these and other new business models are being tested.

One approach is to consider what would happen if one person were removed and what the consequences would be for the business. If that person fulfils a useful role, one that you know little about, then that absence would require someone else to do that job, reducing his capacity to do the job he already has.

Of course, some lawyers live in a world in which there is infinite capacity for the business to meet their needs because all they need do is create drama and demand attention to get what they want done. The corollary of infinite capacity is infinite deferral, which means that whatever was being done before resources were diverted to a new "priority" is deferred until resources once again become available. Such people don't understand why others become frustrated as their needs are, for them at least, clearly paramount.

There are many forms of equality—for example, that we are all equal before the law and in death. One of the great challenges of equality in the context of business, and in the context of legal practice, is that we generally don't want to be equal. What we want is to be more powerful and better rewarded than others. So long as we are not one of the more powerful and better rewarded, we strive to become one of them. While I am not decrying ambition, there is an insidious tendency, particularly prevalent in law firms, to put others down in order to get ahead. If this sort of behaviour is rewarded by advancement, the inevitable result is that the wrong people become leaders and the cycle persists.

When it comes to reward, there is always discussion and comparison of contribution. If practice were only concerned with hours billed, and every practice were only manned by partners agreeing to partition income only by reference to their own hours billed, things would be pretty straightforward. However, running and building a practice are generally more complex activities and involve contributions that cannot be measured in terms of chargeable time.

Each of us has a particular contribution to make in the context of the circumstances and opportunities presented to us each day. Science has shown that we are each subject to cycles that affect us physiologically and psychologically; we naturally experience times of expansion and contraction (and I do not mean of the waist line). From one day to the next, and often from one moment to the next, we are less or more capable, less or more competent to fulfil what is expected.

There is never equality of contribution, though there may be equality in contribution. By this I mean that, if we are willing to measure contribution in terms other than financial, then we can readily draw the conclusion that it is possible for everyone to contribute fully without each contribution ever being precisely the same as others. If we accept this proposition, then we consider a legal practice, much like a team engaged in a sport, to be an enterprise in which partners and others make their individual contributions only by reference to the whole.

The performance of the whole practice is by definition dependent on the contribution of each individual. The contribution of each individual is also necessary to realize the whole. No one is therefore redundant; all should be treated as equally important within the business, or to the business, until a conscious decision is made otherwise.

To make any change to the contribution of an individual is necessarily to change the practice as a whole. The individual can change the way in which she contributes (as opposed to a formal change in role, function, or practice area). Such changes would include changes in behaviour, attitude, communication, and relationship. If the individual changes, then, however subtly, the whole practice has changed. The individual remains relevant as part of a coherent whole and equal in contribution.

Should the firm, through its management, decide that an individual is no longer relevant, there can no longer be equality in contribution. Unless and until that happens, the individual remains relevant and therefore important in her way and should be regarded and treated as such by others. Unfortunately, what happens in practice is that individual partners and others decide unilaterally that a particular individual is not equal in contribution; this is the most common source of divisiveness undermining coherence and cohesion.

The managing partner of a London firm who read through an ownership and reward model I had devised told me gleefully that he had found the flaw in my scheme: namely, he believed that some partners needed to be treated "more equally" than others. This person clearly enjoyed his power of patronage too much to surrender it to transparency. If everyone is equal in contribution, then they should be treated as such. This is not to say that the criteria for financial reward may not allow for variance in the level of reward. What matters is that the criteria be transparent, reflect contributions made to the practice beyond billable hours, and be demonstrably fair not only among the partners but throughout the firm.

One argument commonly presented for providing excessive reward to individual partners is that they could earn more money elsewhere. In my view, if a partner sees himself as an independent business operating in the context of the legal practice, then it is only right that he might choose to maximize revenues to that business—his business. If, on the other hand, a partner recognizes value derived from participation in the practice as a whole, then it is that value that becomes of paramount importance. If a partner feels that he is not being paid enough for what he does, then there are likely to be many other issues that lie beneath that concern to be addressed; money is seldom the real issue.

The non-financial rewards of practice, of participation in a collective endeavour, are the rewards that we need not do without. However, in order to enjoy them we need a different way of seeing our contribution and the contributions of others.

HIRING

Another area that requires so little effort and yet can demonstrate consideration for others is that of dealing with applicants seeking positions with your firm. Whether you are dealing with an applicant directly or working through a headhunter or a recruitment firm, it is important to show consideration for the interests of the applicant. If contact is badly handled, the message received is extremely negative and not quickly forgotten.

If you invite applications for any position in your firm, whether it is through advertising, through a standing instruction to recruiters, or in the careers section of your website, all applicants should be treated with the respect they deserve for responding to your invitation. It is, after all, your invitation. You are asking someone else to take the time to respond to your need to fill a particular position. You are asking applicants to submit applications and to attend interviews with all the time and emotional investment that demands.

If you take the view that you are the one doing the favour—the one who is graciously offering an opportunity that anyone should be glad to have—then your arrogance will obscure better judgment and you will behave accordingly. Take a moment to ask yourself honestly what your attitude is when it comes to recruitment. If you feel prideful, then have a serious talk with yourself; it is simply unkind and ungracious to dish out humiliation to others.

Many who apply may not be suitably qualified, yet every one of them will be seeking a job that will allow them at least to make a living and at best to give their lives further meaning and purpose. Whether they are out of work, or in a job that for one reason or another is not right for them, applying for a new a job involves taking the risk of rejection, and this is hard for anyone to do. Recruitment is a situation that cries out for empathy.

When you receive an application, the very first thing to do is to give an acknowledgment (see Chapter 11). Even if the application has come through a recruiter, ensure that an acknowledgment is sent to the applicant stating when you will respond with a decision whether or not to take the application further. Then make sure that you get back to the applicant on or before the time that you said you would.

When an applicant is going through the interview stages, it is important to show the same courtesies that you would expect someone to extend to you. Do not justify or explain away delays with the excuse of partners being unavailable to make decisions. All partners bear responsibility for the dealings that the firm has with others, including applicants. A firm that makes such excuses is effectively saying that its partners operate independently of the firm and without accountability or responsibility for the firm's undertaking of recruitment. This is plainly nonsense, yet it goes on all the time. That doesn't make it right.

If the applicant is not suitable, then please make the effort to tell the applicant that you are not able to take the application further, explaining in general terms why that is; then express sincere good wishes for the applicant's success in finding a suitable position and in their future career. Essentially, write the kind of letter that you would like to receive, or would like a friend or family member to receive. Please do not say that you will keep the application on file—this insults the intelligence of any applicant.

A well-handled refusal will leave one more person out there ready to speak well of your firm. Think of all the applicants who, with a little effort, can be rewarded, encouraged, and, despite their rejection, will be likely to have only good things to say about your firm. You never know, one of them might end up as one of your most important clients. That which goes around, comes around.

When I was looking to transfer to London for the balance of my traineeship, I applied to a number of recruitment firms, including one whose letter to me I have never forgotten. They told me that I simply did not have anything to offer that any of their clients might be remotely interested in. I went on to find a position with Lovells, who thought otherwise. Many years later, when I was running my own firm, that recruitment firm contacted me, wanting our business. I turned them down and explained precisely why; I don't know if it did any good, but I hoped that the organization might think twice before treating other applicants in the same way.

Treating people as a commodity, as so many dispensable and replaceable units of expense, is regrettably still the norm in too many businesses, including professional firms. The way in which a firm handles its applicants reflects the way it handles its people. If you don't like the way a firm is dealing with you as an applicant, be warned.

FIRING

This is an aspect of practice management that deserves careful attention and conduct. I am not talking here about employment law obligations but about what matters most when bringing an end to a relationship involving any member of your firm: the human issues that deserve personal attention and consideration.

Being fired, let go, terminated, made redundant—or whatever term is used to describe it—is an extremely painful experience for anyone to have to go through. The sense of rejection, abandonment, and loss of community and belonging are always present, however well disguised. It is hard enough for some people to decide that they must move on voluntarily, leaving behind colleagues and shared experience. To be forced to leave, to be told that you are no longer wanted, is to experience social exclusion.

Of course, it is necessary to fire people from your business when conditions demand it. There may be many reasons: gross misconduct, negative behaviours, poor performance. Whatever the reason, there is also cause. Each person you fire came into the business as a new recruit selected for his or her skills, personality, experience, and qualifications. Something has happened to change that, and it is important to be clear that you and the person you are firing understand what that is.

Unfortunately, individuals are often singled out for one reason or another, perhaps by a partner or even by a peer, and gradually that individual loses favour and others consider him "not one of us." This happens wherever a blame culture prevails, where ostracism is the consequence of others distancing themselves from responsibility. People can all too often behave like the body's immune system, surrounding and attacking anything it finds to be alien or possibly malign.

The decision to fire someone should never be easy because it should involve asking tough questions about what you and others could have done, what conditions of support and encouragement could have been provided, that could have allowed the person concerned to fulfil their true potential within the organization. One of my erstwhile partners was fond of the phrase: "When you point your finger at someone, there are always three fingers pointing back at you." This is a maxim that is easy to repeat but demands considerable personal strength and honesty.

A lot of people are fired simply because people in charge don't like them. As the thinker thinks, the prover proves—so reasons are found. This happens in any organization and, however sophisticated we think we are, however meticulous law makers have been in seeking to protect employees against unfairness, too many still make decisions that affect others based on very basic instincts and primitive behaviour.

I have fired many good people and, barring one or two occasions, each time I found it very difficult to do; I'm glad I did. Undoubtedly, I made mistakes, and many of the people concerned may still harbour resentment and have had to deal with feelings of betrayal, which I have come to know personally and in the most profound way. That said, hard decisions are made in the interest of the "greater good." We must simply be careful how we rationalize what that greater good is.

Recognizing that the experience of being fired is going to be emotionally painful, I believe that everything should be done to demonstrate respect for the person concerned. The fact that you consider the individual no longer to be of value to your firm does not mean that you need not value their humanity. To sincerely recognize the value in each individual is to honour him or her, and that makes you honourable. From this recognition can spring the confidence that everyone needs to carry on and sustain a sense of self-worth.

In my view, firing someone is a job for the most senior member of the firm appropriate for the person concerned. It is not something to be left to an office manager or HR manager, insulating those who have ordered the termination from facing the individual concerned. To do so fails to recognize the importance of what is being done, both to the individual and the firm. To do so is to miss an opportunity to show respect and kindness, to the detriment of everyone concerned.

CLIENT CARE

This is a term that has become part of the vocabulary of regulation. There are client care rules governing the responsibilities that lawyers have towards their clients, including the way in which we communicate with them; the kind of information we are obliged to provide; the manner in which we will handle taking on new instructions, handling complaints, and termination of instructions; and so on.

There are also client care letters that have become a means by which the lawyer distances himself from his client, establishing the ground rules as to how any challenge or complaint will be dealt with. Unfortunately, the result of these elaborate regulations and procedures is that lawyers seem in the process to lose their sense of what is right and what is proportionate in handling a client relationship. They revert instead to digging in behind the ramparts of client care provisions.

Client care is about making sure that your clients understand what is going on and what you're saying to them, and it's about caring whether they feel truly in control of their situations in the context of their relationships with you. It is not enough to be accurate or to be right if the client does not understand what is going on.

As lawyers, we develop a language that is all our own. Very few outside the law find it easy to listen to us when we are speaking "professionally"; we have a tendency to use language in a way that is simply not familiar to those outside the practice of law. In the name of clarity, we all too often deliver obscurity. This is a particular issue when writing to clients. Far too many letters go out containing vast amounts of information and workmanlike summaries of the law but with little in the way of clear recommendations that make sense within the client's frame of reference.

Client care requires that you sincerely engage with your client's interests. The term *client's interest* is too often used these days to explain the actions of professional advisers that are, in fact, in their own interests and not those of the client. If you want to know what your client's interests are at any one time, you have to ask, listen, and comprehend. A client's ideas about a desirable outcome may vary from time to time as circumstances and perceptions change. We have to be sure not to make assumptions and to always inquire of clients whether they consider any proposed action to be genuinely in their interests. I think it's right to ask why a client wants to take a particular course and be sure you understand what they hope to gain from it. You can only manage expectations if you know what they are.

Client care involves compassion and empathy. At the same time, an essential distance needs to be observed and respected between individuals, allowing each to experience his or her own reality. A willingness to understand and have respect for what a client is experiencing is something that enriches the service experience for the lawyer and for the client.

Rather than setting standards for what is most convenient to you in terms of your methods of working and preferences in terms of communication, is it not better to ask the client how he would like to be communicated with? In this way the client can work with you to establish the channels and frequency of communication that meet the client's individual needs for information and reassurance. Of course, a balance has to be struck, but it should lean towards the side of communicating well and not towards serving the lawyer's purposes.

More time spent in communication may well mean more costs; this should be the choice of the client. Keeping in touch with your client the way that the client prefers is the most likely means by which the client will come to perceive a favourable service experience, one that the client will hopefully wish to repeat and report to others. Not doing so is a certain way to undermine your efforts to be appreciated for doing a good job. It may seem perverse and unfair to a lawyer that his efforts should go unmarked, but if he has not communicated with the client, then how would the client know of what he has done?

In-house counsel have their own particular communication needs. They report within their own organizations, dealing with the different personalities and expectations within their company. Your communications with them and your management of their expectations are all they have to work with in order to manage, in turn, their relationships with decision-makers and colleagues.

Finding out to how your client prefers to communicate can pay enormous dividends. Once you have established channels and methods of communication that genuinely work, they will perceive their relationship with you to be easier than their relationships with others (who insist instead on their own preferred methods of communication). They simply find it easier to deal with someone who is willing to interact in the way that they find most helpful.

Of course, it is important to have boundaries. The relationship with the client is one of client and adviser, based not only on professional duty but also on service. "Client care" as represented by the client care letter is not about service; it is simply a euphemism for terms and conditions. Real care is demonstrated by sincere interest and the willingness to be flexible and adaptive towards the needs of others. These principles are not to be set aside in a professional relationship but rather used to make such relationships enduring and rewarding beyond mere economic return.

Fear of complaint changes behaviour, invariably bringing about the thing that is feared. Undue formality and distance, exhibited in so many different ways in the course of communication, does nothing to protect the lawyer from complaint and only increases the likelihood of that occurring. Lawyers need to soften their approach in order to have more meaningful personal relationships with their clients as human beings rather than as adversaries. In his book *Blink*, Malcolm Gladwell refers to research carried out in the United States revealing that doctors and surgeons who behave considerately towards their patients, take the time to understand their needs, and have a good "bedside manner" are far less likely to be sued for negligence. I suspect the same applies to lawyers.

Once you have embedded a good and healthy attitude towards client care, you will discover that there are myriad ways in which that care can be expressed, often through a multitude of little acts that together add up to great service.

Summary

- Valuing others opens up relationship and involves looking for the value that every relationship holds for you and the value that you can contribute to it

- Appreciation has real impact on the receiver when sincerely offered, provided time is given to convey your acknowledgement and gratitude for their contribution

- Reassurance rekindles enthusiasm, restores commitment, and establishes loyalty

- Being valued is important to everyone and proper recognition encourages contributions that are not directly measurable in terms of revenue but nonetheless impact the bottom line

- The highest and lowest paid in an organization are deserving of the same respect as they are equal in making their individual contributions, each important in their way to the business and therefore to each other

- Hiring new people is something that should be handled considerately, respecting the investment applicants make and risks they take in answering your invitation to apply

- Firing someone should not be undertaken lightly and handled with consideration and respect for the individual by the most senior person appropriate

- Client care is much more than a regulatory requirement and involves genuine enquiry into what works best for a client, particularly in terms of communication

- Real care is demonstrated by sincere interest and the willingness to be flexible and adaptive towards the needs of others

- Lawyers need to improve their 'bedside' manner and not retreat into formality whether driven by fear of recrimination or simply to avoid personal contact

- Great service experience is the result of the often small but important ways in which a client is made to feel valued

Collaboration

The urge to compete is one of the many urges we feel as human beings and is one whose force can be channelled in a creative and inclusive way or exploited for selfish gain. *Competitiveness* has sadly become synonymous with ruthlessness—with negative and destructive behaviours justified by financial performance and apologist mantras such as "increasing shareholder value."

Competition for the individual lawyer is present from day one. The road ahead to partnership is so clearly one that favours the strong and cannot favour all. Not to become a partner is to fail; to be passed over is a rejection that few completely recover from. From the very beginning, favour is sought and favourites are established among partners in a tradition of patronage that is self-perpetuating and divisive.

If you can show yourself to be smarter, better, quicker than the others, then you will be chosen, applauded, and rewarded. If you can look good or make those more senior than you look good, then your success will be noted; if you help your peers to succeed, then they will claim that success for themselves rather than give you credit for your contribution. This is the kind of thinking that predominates in a command and control culture in which leadership encourages the hungry to fight for scraps to prove who is worthy, just as they had to do.

There is another kind of competition, one in which the individual and the firm compete against the limitations on their capacity for excellence, coherence, and service. Taking this approach to competition, we do not seek to deny or diminish the qualities of others but to enhance our own. This form of competition is every bit as challenging and, in practice, more constructive and sustainable. I firmly believe that if you get it right, the money comes—in other words, if you focus wholeheartedly on service, then opportunities for service will arise and the financial rewards will follow.

In his autobiography, US Secretary of State Colin Powell refers to a precept by which he has sought to live and work: "excellence should not be an exception but a prevailing attitude." Excellence in service is a constantly moving target; there is always room for incremental improvement. Just as it would be nonsense to think that we have fully evolved as human beings, it is equally unlikely that we have achieved anything close to our full potential as legal professionals and providers of legal services. There is plenty of room for growth in ways that do not necessarily include profit, but that do not preclude it either.

If you believe that traditional internal competition is the best way to drive performance in your firm, then that is the culture you will create. I want to suggest that there is another way: one that is conducive to an experience of success that is more rewarding, more sustainable, and based in collaboration as opposed to competition. Collaboration begins, as in all things, with intention and is sustained through positive attitude. If you can establish the right "state of mind" within yourself, then your intention and attitude will be collaborative and you will know what to do, how to act, how to collaborate. Collaboration is the expression of a collaborative ethos.

In his letter to the Philippians, St. Paul described precisely the kind of attitude that is required for collaboration:

> If our life in Christ means anything to you, if love can persuade at all, or the spirit that we have in common, or any tenderness and sympathy, then be united in your convictions and united in your love, with a common purpose and a common mind. That is the one thing that would make me completely happy. There must be no competition among you, no conceit; but everybody is to be self-effacing. Always consider the other person to be better than yourself, so that nobody thinks of his own interests first but everybody thinks of other people's interests instead.

If you want people to be united, with a "common purpose and a common mind," then this is precisely the kind of behaviour that has to be encouraged and conspicuously displayed, beginning with those in leadership.

INTERDEPENDENCE

What is vital to success, whether in personal or professional relationships, is recognizing and honouring of the truth of interdependence. Hierarchy tends, as history shows all too clearly, to encourage those in power, those at the top, to forget that they cannot be at the top of anything unless there are others willing to take their place in the lower echelons. Power corrupts when it causes the individual to forget the interdependence that exists between them and those over whom they have authority. To ignore this interdependence is to fail to understand the fundamental reality that everyone engaged in business is so by individual consent, which can be withdrawn at any time.

In his teaching through the organization Psychology of Vision, Chuck Spezzano defines three stages a business may pass through in the course of its development. The first stage is that of dependence. The business is growing into its adolescence, during which time it is highly dependent on staff members and on client relationships, and it struggles for financial security.

The next stage is that of independence, during which the business becomes more aware of its own power and begins to fear losing what it has gained, leading its behaviours to change. It becomes more focused on retaining what it has rather than continuing to grow and evolve.

It is then only with clarity and vision that the business can move into interdependence and "mastery." In this condition of interdependence, it flourishes and grows while recognizing and embracing the importance of cooperation and collaboration both within itself and outside itself, in the form of its relationships with its clients, complimentary service providers, and even competitors. It is perfectly possible for a fledgling law firm to step straight into mastery provided that those in leadership determine from the outset that stated values will be expressed in every aspect of the business.

One way of looking at interdependence is to consider within your own office which person might be judged to be the least important, whether according to rank or income. Then consider how your business would operate today if you were to remove from it that most junior person, the one with the least authority, the lowest paid. That person might be an administrative assistant, a receptionist, a cleaner. If you look deeply into this, you see that the business will experience an immediate contraction, however slight, placing pressure on everyone else to one degree or another. In fact, it can be the seemingly lowliest members of a firm who are most missed when they are absent. Everyone is replaceable, whether in the short or long term, including individual lawyers and owners. Would you prefer to work in a business in which everyone is considered important to the business or one where no one is?

If a person is not important or relevant to the business, then that person is redundant and should no longer be in it. If, however, that person is not redundant, then that importance cannot be underestimated or undervalued without there being consequences, however subtle, to the collective force and effectiveness of your business. If you start to look at everyone in your business in this way, if you start to see them all as important in their own way, then your behaviour towards them and your consideration of them will necessarily change for the better. If you engage sincerely in this process, it may lead you to reassess the working conditions and expectations affecting everyone within the business. A reassessment of these matters might, I suggest, lead to you bringing about changes that will have an overall and lasting beneficial effect on business that will, in turn, produce the revenues and professional success that you desire.

ONE BUSINESS OR A "BUSINESS OF ONE"

The partnership model is one that for most has little to do with the notion of partnership as used in common language; the focus is rather on liability and taxation. Partners are bound for only so long as it serves each one and for the purpose of sharing in control and profits. There may be genuine friendship between some and loyalty of a sort among others; the larger the firm, the more fertile the ground for dissent and disassociation. There is a tension present in most partnerships that centres on "contribution" measured in financial terms or in seniority, and it becomes a source of resentment and envy.

Election to partnership is usually based on the individual's capacity to contribute to revenues without reducing existing partners' profit shares. If you are being promoted from within the firm, then you may have been able to secure some clients of your own if partners have allowed you to do so. If you are joining from outside the firm, then you will be expected to have a "following"; this refers to the portfolio of clients and value of client business that you may be able to transport from one firm to another.

The hallmark of a successful lawyer in this system is the ability to gather a number and a certain value of clients who can be migrated to another firm. To achieve this, it is necessary to develop close personal relationships with such clients and cultivate the impression that only you understand their work and business needs. This means "looking after them" and making sure that no one else is doing so (if clients are to deal with others, then making sure that those are associates and that you can step in to "sort things out" and grab all the credit).

One practice commonly encouraged by leadership is "cross-selling." The idea behind cross-selling is that one should ensure that clients who contract with the firm in one service area are made aware of other services also offered by the firm and encouraged to use them. In practice within this system, this involves partners doing something potentially damaging to their personal interests, their bargaining power within the firm, and their value to any firm they may in future wish to join. Cross-selling is made all the more difficult when, as is invariably the case, partners consider most of their peers to be less able than they are, and therefore likely to disappoint the client, who may well then blame the introducing partner.

When a "lateral hire" is brought into the firm, and perhaps favoured with special terms to clinch the deal, this immediately causes others to wonder what their worth might be in terms of their own "following" and renew efforts to secure that ground. Should anyone be surprised when that same lateral hire maintains a carefully monitored no-fly zone around his or her clients and later moves off again, taking those followers and perhaps more?

If a partner leaves a firm, usually the first concern is to consider how to enforce restrictive covenants and prevent the loss of client business in the face of an act of blatant disloyalty. In the same moment, the firm will be retaining recruitment firms and placing advertising for the vacancy, requiring from the lucky candidate a following; in other words, they will expect that the candidate will somehow overcome any covenant, behave disloyally towards their current partners, and ultimately achieve what the departing partner is, if possible, to be prevented from doing.

A more integrated business approach that treats clients as being clients of the firm, for which everyone in the firm has responsibility, is one that is more likely to build sustainable service relationships and so build value in the organization (as opposed to building the "celebrity" of individual partners). A firm united in common purpose and by shared values has the capacity to grow as a unit and from itself as a whole rather than primarily through acquisition.

A firm that operates as an integrated business looks for contribution from a partner that goes far beyond a "book of business." Such contribution would include the partner's ability to nurture talent within the firm, management experience, professional and business acumen, communications skills, innovation, marketing experience, creativity, and leadership.

A healthy business is able to retain earnings for investment in training and education, technology and communications, market research, and service product development. The rest of the business world is generally bemused and often frustrated by the unwillingness of the legal profession to evolve, to adopt technology, to deliver real efficiencies, to fundamentally improve services. So long as no one changes, there is no choice, and the legal profession can stay as it is, at least until there is some catalyst that forces change.

That catalyst has perhaps now arrived in various forms, including alternative business structures; deregulation that is opening up new service markets in what is known as "legal tech"; and the growing acceptance of so-called "unbundling" of legal services, in which lawyers do what only they can do, leaving the rest to be done by the client or ancillary service providers who can do the work for less than a law firm would charge.

Change, when it really takes hold, will force firms to address imbalances in the traditional ownership and reward system, which will bring the legal profession into its next phase of development and closer to modern business.

Summary

- There is a great deal of divisive internal competition within traditional law firms, encouraged by fear-based 'command and control' management

- Collaboration is more necessary than ever and yet traditional culture militates against it

- Instead of competing with each other, it is better to focus on competing to overcome limitations on excellence in service

- Collaboration is a result of collaborative ethos and involves uniting everyone with a common purpose and a common mind, competing collectively towards excellence in service

- The ability to recognize the essential interdependencies that allow your business to flourish is essential to creating and maintaining a collaborative culture

- Collaborative culture has to be demonstrated by those in leadership (the 'Partners') who have a tendency to think of themselves as a 'business of one'

- Partners are invariably ranked and rewarded by reference to the client revenues and relationships that are seen to belong to them

- Self-interest leads Partners to covet and protect what they regard as theirs and that they know will be valuable to any business they might move to, including a new firm of their own

- Lateral hiring, as opposed to promoting to Partner from within, is a quick way of growing a firm and yet doing so reinforces the tendency of Partners to ring fence their 'following'

- Choosing a more integrated 'one business' approach can only be achieved by revisiting traditional ownership and reward structures

Blame Culture

If we could read the secret history of our enemies,
we should find in each man's life sorrow and
suffering enough to disarm all hostility.
—*Henry Wadsworth Longfellow*

Blame is fundamentally different from responsibility; taking responsibility and taking the blame are worlds apart. Blame is an endemic condition that persists in organizations, small and large, in which express or implied permission is given for the process by which one or more individuals are singled out to bear alone the consequences of some action or inaction that is deemed to have caused harm to the business.

Just as every human action can be said to be motivated by the avoidance of shame, so too is every effort made to avoid blame. Blame is the allocation of shame and invariably involves a scapegoat punished for the misdeeds of others. Blame is something that people learn, much like bullying, from those in power whose example is followed and who learned it from those who taught them as they grew up in their professional lives. Blame culture feeds on itself through a continuous cycle of fear and retribution, and it is this cycle that must be consciously broken if true responsibility is ever to be allowed to take its place.

The fear of being blamed for some failure, large or small, invariably leads to stress and pressure being forced downward through the hierarchy of a firm, to the detriment of everyone. This atmosphere of fear then creates the conditions for further errors and blame. A culture of blame encourages concealment and blame-shifting, which fundamentally undermines previously harmonious relationships.

In an organization where a culture of blame prevails, that organization learns nothing from mistakes, however they occurred. Such organizations overreact to events that give rise to blame and seek to impose ever more rigorous controls rather than trying to understand how such mistakes arose and what, at the deepest level, caused one or more individuals to lose their normal focus and attention. Such organizations are at pains to be seen to be taking action in order not to be blamed for failing to do so.

Blamed individuals are isolated and thereby subjected to shame. While those in leadership may refer to their sense of responsibility, the very process of blame is one that causes separation and detachment rather than an embrace of errors as shared by the whole business and everyone in it. By comparison, everyone endeavours to share in success. It is not unlike profit and loss: everyone wants a share of profits; few are willing to share in losses.

Sharing in mistakes means sharing the responsibility for understanding precisely what gave rise to a particular set of circumstances, or situation, or outcome. Even where an error has arisen due to a simple human failure to give attention to a particular matter (for example, placing the wrong letter into an addressed envelope), the first thing is to recognize that the error is one that could equally well have been made by you in the same or similar circumstances. If you start from the point of view that a mistake is something completely alien to you, as something which has never and could never occur in your reality, then you are not only separating yourself, you are kidding yourself. Most importantly, you will be unable to empathize with the person who has made a mistake or help that person to learn from it. A mistake is an opportunity for learning, both for the person who makes the mistake and for those who work with or have delegated responsibility to that person. Mistakes can reveal opportunities.

In any business, and even among its leadership, mistakes will happen; sometimes as a result of the actions or inactions of those in leadership and, more commonly, among those who are answerable to leadership. It is more likely that staff will make mistakes than that leaders will simply because there are usually many more of them engaged in those aspects of the day-to-day conduct of the business in which mistakes can be made.

It is necessary to delegate and share with staff the responsibility for carrying out the purposes of the business. In this way, support staff can be seen as an extension of you as a leader, part of you and your consciousness. Such staff are there to represent your business and, in so doing, represent you. To blame them when errors occur is to suggest that this relationship does not, in fact, exist and that you are not, in fact, responsible; that it is not, in fact, you or the extended you that has made the mistake. Telling a client that someone else made the mistake so as to distance yourself from it never goes down well; it sends entirely the wrong message.

Any good person is going to feel very badly about having made a mistake and you will add only to the pain and shame they experience by adding insult to their injury. In the moment the individual realizes that he has made a mistake, he is extremely vulnerable and at that point is open to suggestion and direction. Handle the situation badly, through abuse, blame, or recrimination, and that person will close up and submit to one degree or another to whatever is imposed by way of punishment. That person will then repeat that behaviour with others who make mistakes. Handle it well and you will imprint on that individual permission to behave with compassion and understanding and so earn the loyalty that you deserve as well as ensure that it is paid forward.

It is the nature of blame culture to ignore the simple fact that mistakes are made and will be made. This due to the nature of the work, the opportunity for misunderstanding and error in communications between people, and the competing pressures for attention placed on everyone in a professional business. I was once told by Ian Jenkins, then senior partner of Barlow Lyde & Gilbert, a firm in which I worked that specialized in dealing with professional negligence, that mistakes were inevitable. His stated wish was that my mistakes would be small ones and that I would always feel able to come to him and tell him about them so that we could solve them together in order to minimize any consequent harm to the firm and its clients. This, in my view, is the right approach and a valued lesson I have tried to pass on.

People who have made mistakes and then been handled with consideration and compassion will replicate that behaviour in turn with others who are responsible to them. This is a virtuous cycle of behaviour that sustains and builds the individual and collective energy within a firm. It also encourages openness and creativity in finding solutions to problems that arise and ensuring that everybody works together to learn and to implement such changes as are necessary to reduce the risk of future problems arising. This, in turn, improves the overall performance of the firm by managing risk through consent and awareness rather than through sanction and retribution. Risk, like change, is not an option.

Blame is essentially an expression of fear. Fear undermines our ability to think and act clearly and intelligently. Blame engenders fear and causes fear to proliferate. Blame is not productive. Blame disguises and conceals. Blame alienates and separates. Blame is the natural born killer of community, cooperation, and collaboration. Blame is denial of the inescapable reality of human error. Blame is a form of control in that its purpose is to contain and create distance from responsibility.

Blame involves judgment. Judgment sets and fixes responsibility without sharing in responsibility. Blame is an excuse and avoidance of the responsibility that should be absorbed collectively and put to good purpose to advance and evolve the competence and maturity of the firm. As you can probably tell, I do not like blame. I don't like to be the subject of blame nor do I like to impose it on others. I have too often imposed it on myself and experienced the negative consequences of that choice.

RESPONSIBILITY

Responsibility is the ability to provide a response as opposed to reacting to any given situation. It is the capacity to recognize that the situation is just that—a situation—and no more than that. Taking responsibility in a conscious and compassionate way is to place a given set of circumstances in perspective and context. Responsibility is also the ability to act intelligently in order to resolve the issue, to learn from it, and to move forward stronger as an individual and more cohesive as a group than you were before.

When a problem arises, it is all too easy to become hysterical and to imagine the possible consequences. These extrapolations are unlikely to occur, and they inflate and often distort the true meaning of what has occurred. This tendency is always more prevalent in a culture of blame. The philosopher Nietzsche said, "That which does not kill us makes us stronger." Problems come and go in the life of any business. Understand the mutual interests that support continuity of the business and recognize how your business and others have ridden waves and lived on to grow and prosper.

Responsibility does not indulge in melodrama. In a culture that promotes responsibility, problems are treated as opportunities to learn, to mature, and to develop individually and collectively. There are, in the end, very few problems that cannot be solved. It is well to remember this when confronting any issue that may arise in the course of your day. The rejection and alienation that is so common in a culture of blame serves no one, least of all the business. It serves only to restrict individual and collective energy by instilling fear and undermining the confidence essential to promoting cooperation and flow in a business. Choose instead to be responsible and act accordingly.

Summary

- Every one of us does our utmost to avoid shame as it is the commonly accepted to be the lowest form of human experience

- Blame is the allocation of shame to one or more individuals held accountable for some failure, loss or other negative outcome

- Blame is essentially an expression of fear and undermines our ability to think and act clearly and intelligently

- A firm with a blame culture leads people to find every means possible to avoid being blamed, including concealing errors and omissions

- Sharing in mistakes means sharing the responsibility for understanding what gave rise to them and integrating that learning into the organization

- Mistakes are inevitable and sharing in responsibility for addressing them, however minor or otherwise, allows individuals and so the organization to move forward with confidence

- When leaders share in responsibility they eschew melodrama and embrace learning for the good of all

10

Conditions for Change

There are a number of key conditions for change, for personal and organizational growth, that, once established, allow you and colleagues in your organization to flourish through change rather than flounder. These are commitment, readiness, attitude, intention, direction, and energy. These conditions are constantly in play, underpinning performance and promoting confidence.

COMMITMENT

Commitment is something I have always considered important. I thought I knew when I had it and when others did not. I could recognize commitment when I saw it—or at least thought I could. However, after throwing myself so wholeheartedly into so many things over so many years, and encouraging others to do the same, I have come to what I believe is a better and more practical definition of what commitment can mean for each of us.

Commitment is commonly used to refer to how much time you are putting in to something—in the case of a lawyer, the number of hours (preferably billable). It is evidenced by the degree to which you have given up other things to devote yourself predominantly or exclusively to one thing. When lawyers talk about wanting to see commitment, they are usually referring to giving up personal needs and priorities for the firm; for example, a lawyer who wants to spend time with a young family may be said to not show the "right level of commitment."

One thing that has become clear to me is that sacrifice has no place in commitment. Sacrifice is corrosive and eats away at you until the pain is so great that you lash out or seek escape from the object of reluctant duty. It is said that to get something, you have to give something up. Sacrifice is like pretending to give something up but never truly doing so; for example, forgoing a chance for revenge instead of truly forgiving. Asking others to make sacrifices, as I have done in the past, is wrong and unfair. True commitment is something that can only be given freely.

Commitment is a condition in which you are confident that you are where you are meant to be; that you are in the business, or in the relationship, that is right for you at this moment. To commit is to acknowledge the choice that you have made and to believe that, for this moment, it is the right one. Commitment creates the space within which it is possible to find motivation and fulfilment.

Commitment is to give oneself wholeheartedly to something or to someone. When we speak of giving our heart to something we are speaking about far more than a purely intellectual process. We are describing an emotional investment, one in which we have placed our emotional energy. The decision to apply ourselves is not a purely rational one; it is deeply intuitive. When our heart is in something our energy flows freely; when it is not, we are constricted and less able, or even unable, to bring all our resources to bear.

Just think of how circumstances are made easier by acknowledging them as they are. We constantly find ourselves in situations we would rather not be in. The natural reaction of the mind is to put up resistance, to complain. This resistance takes up available resources and causes stress. Resistance prevents you from participating in what is going on or gaining even the smallest benefit from it. The choices you may have available to you are to remove yourself from the situation or to accept it as it is and take what you can from it until you are able to make a change.

If your mind takes over, then you can find yourself so quickly submerged in self-criticism ("Why did I put myself in this position?") or criticism of others ("Why did he/she/they put me in this position?"). If, on the other hand, you try saying to yourself, "I am precisely where I am meant to be," then you have immediately relieved yourself of the mental chatter and recrimination underpinned by feelings of insecurity. You can then either give attention to what is going on to perhaps gain something from it, or remove yourself from the situation, accepting the consequences of so doing.

Commitment is a conscious condition and one that can only be truly established and refreshed through awareness. There is no better way to start the day at work than to be able to look around and say to yourself, "I know why I am working here today. This is the business in which I am welcome. This is the career in which I belong." If you are able to say this, or something like it, during the course of any day, then you are experiencing commitment and have the power to give yourself wholeheartedly to whatever you do.

In a state of commitment, there is no part of your being and no portion of your energy that is withheld or directed elsewhere. Your mind is not engaged in resistance, complaining, fantasizing, or constructing schemes by which to avoid or escape the present. You are in a state of preparedness. You are ready for motivation to direct your energy to a particular purpose, objective, or goal in the context and for the benefit of the business in which you are working. Motivation is specific and active. Commitment is the space within which motivation can exist.

Commitment is an intensely personal matter and cannot be forced; it is either there or it isn't. Motivation, or at least what looks like motivation, can be forced through fear, threats, and bullying. Professional organizations that rely on this kind of motivation, as all too many do, are simply not utilizing the potential contributions of their members. So if commitment is a precondition for true motivation, how then to engender commitment? The answer lies in self-management and in recognizing that very few of us are able to establish and maintain commitment without support and encouragement.

In professional relationships, just as in personal relationships, every opportunity should be taken to reinforce and reassure the other. There is great benefit to be gained from revisiting the nature and intent of the relationship. Doing so can clear the decks of minor causes of disaffection and dissatisfaction, bringing back into focus and perspective the importance and validity of the relationship. I will explore later how this may be done, but do it you must, for yourself and others, if you want to achieve and sustain commitment.

In professional business, every member of a firm or group comes to work each day as an individual wrestling with their humanity and beset to one degree or another by fear and uncertainty. It is not enough to assume that because someone took the job they are possessed of an absolute conviction and commitment to the firm and to their work. It would also be wrong to assume that someone who has become a partner or owner, or who holds some position of authority or leadership, is necessarily also always possessed of such conviction and commitment.

Take time to reinforce in every member of a professional group the values and objectives that bind the group together. This does not mean simply rehearsing what is presented in the careers section of your website. It involves, as often as possible or necessary, talking about what is important to the individual in the context of what is important for the organization. The ideal conditions for commitment will exist where there is an alignment between the values of the individual and those of the organization (as is explored in Chapter 6).

READINESS

Readiness is a condition of awareness, one in which you are able to bring all of your attention to what will be expected of you; your surroundings and your circumstances, personal and business, are canvas on which the future is made. Readiness is a form of alertness, being alive to all the opportunities that exist for you. It is a state in which you place no immediate limitations on what you may achieve or how you may achieve it. Readiness embraces willingness, an openness to what is and what may be, within which you are willing to create the space to express yourself and to allow others to do so.

One of the coaching methods recommended by Sir John Whitmore, a pioneer of modern business coaching and author of the ground-breaking book, *Coaching for Performance*, is known by the acronym GROW. It consists of goal setting; reality checking the current situation; options for action; and what is to be done, when, by whom, and the will to do it. The will to act is where our true power lies and what moves us from talking about options to following a particular choice.

Lawyers are particularly good at conceptualizing and articulating ideas and options. However, what most are surprisingly reluctant to do is to step into action, particularly where choices have been made collectively. It is as though the old adage that "a lawyer who acts for himself has a fool for a client" also applies to lawyers running their own businesses: confidence and interest are quickly lost as lawyers return to the safety of the treadmill they know rather than participating in change.

When I come to a new challenge, I invariably say to myself, "Everything I have ever done has prepared me for this." I know full well that all I can do is my best and by coaching myself in this way, I give myself confidence that allows me to move freely through the challenge.

ATTITUDE

We are all of us, at almost all times, resolutely engaged in taking a firm hold of the wrong end of the stick. So absorbed are we in the interpretation and evaluation of events as they occur within us that we allow our view of things to infect those events with a meaning that itself becomes a cause of dissatisfaction and disassociation. In Buddhist teaching, it is referred to as the leaning mind, the principal source of all human suffering. This is the nature of the human condition and what we can all safely say we have in common.

Your attitude is your direction. The way you choose to see things is the way they are for you. If you choose to see an opportunity in a set of circumstances, then there is one; if you choose to see failure, then failure is the result. A positive attitude is one that allows for the possibility, indeed anticipates the probability, that you are capable of achieving such objectives as you may set for yourself. An attitude that is not dogged by fear, apprehension, and self-doubt is essential to any change or movement that is to be unrestricted, free, relaxed.

If you have self-belief in your capacity and ability to achieve what you set out to do, then you have provided yourself with the very best platform from which to do so. Attitude is not a blind condition, not one that persuades in the face of all the evidence. Attitude is a condition that recognizes the opportunity and one's potential to achieve it while accepting the inherent responsibility to make the most of the time and circumstances offered to you.

INTENTION

Intention is the formulation of a vision and thereby the creation of a reality that may come into being but is not yet manifest. Intention is an extremely powerful form that can be brought to bear to anticipate a change which, when experienced, is then in a way familiar and thereby easier to absorb and to adapt to. Making an intention is much the same as making a wish, save that your intentions are not left entirely to fate, chance, or a fairy godmother. Instead, you work to bring it about in concert with others.

Intention can, depending on your particular approach, be expressed verbally or through visualization. Visualization is an extremely powerful method to literally *see* how things will be when you have reached the objectives that you wish to attain. That visualization may comprise a whole range of conditions that you would naturally expect to experience when a particular objective is realized. You may, for example, if you are considering expanding your business into a new country, choose to visualize where your office is located, how it is furnished, how many people are in it, what it is like to live and work in that country, and so on.

There are no practical limits to the degree of sophistication with which one can construct an intention. To get the most from this creativity, it is vital to free yourself from the limitations of anxiety, of obstacles internal and external. While it is reasonable to expect obstacles, to anticipate problems and difficulties that may arise, it is equally appropriate to anticipate and prepare for success. In fact, it is of paramount importance to understand what success will look and feel like for you. Once you have a clear picture, you can map that intention against your existing situation and measure where it will take you. Intention is the framing of an idea in such a way as to anticipate its realization.

The challenge, then, is to also understand how others visualize the outcome. It will be important to know how others will measure success once the objective is shared as an experience. This will necessarily involve the map of each individual's set of values, those things that, at one moment in time, those individuals value above others. These values change and evolve just our tastes and preferences do in the course of life. It is therefore entirely possible that the values that are the basis upon which decisions are made at the outset of a period of growth and development may have evolved by the time the objective is achieved.

DIRECTION

Direction is the particular course that is set, not the final destination. To think of growth as a destination is to limit the imagination and to unnecessarily restrict what is an evolutionary process. The experience of direction is the embodiment of readiness, attitude, and intention. It is, in many respects, similar to the notion of purpose. Purpose is often thought of as something determined by a particular outcome: a goal that was achieved. Purpose used in this sense is similar to historical accounting: judging what has happened and assessing one's role by reference to what was achieved.

Purpose, much like direction, is better considered as a way of being rather than as an explanation. Much like happiness, purpose can become something that we continuously postpone to the future. In fact, we can only be happy now, in the present moment, and not in the future. We do not live in the future; we live in the present, so happiness is not something that can be experienced other than now. It is much the same with purpose. Pursuit of purpose requires that we be aware, alert, ready to "fill the unforgiving minute with sixty seconds' worth of distance run" (from Rudyard Kipling's "If"). We share common meaning through self-awareness, and this is a challenge to every one of us in whatever circumstances we find ourselves. Direction is no more, and no less, than the wholehearted pursuit of a clear intention.

What I am trying to convey is the importance of one's state of mind in order to be able to bring about change and growth. If you do not believe that it is possible, if you do not have a clear vision as to what may be possible and have not made a clear decision within yourself to pursue what may be possible, you can have little hope of achieving it.

The process is not one that assumes that you are the prime mover, the sole source of change. I am also not suggesting that the alternative is to be simply carried along by events, to be caught up in the flow of circumstances and simply drawn along by time and tide. What I am suggesting is that there is a combination at work here of both of these facets: the ability to see what is and what may be and simultaneously to allow yourself to move through the flow of time and events in a way that is conscious and allows you to become aware of and seize any opportunities to further your aspirations.

It is, simply put, to know how to keep your head up and look around you to move forward, rather than to "put your head down" to get the work done, only lifting it from time to time when problems arise. What I am describing is a continuous state of readiness, a continuous state in which you are both aware and willing to address what is presented to you in the context of a clear intention (which will allow you to discern which opportunities will further your intention and which will not). You are then in a position to progress by choice and not solely by chance.

By being clear about what you want, your actions and words create an attractive force that fosters the circumstances you require to achieve what you set out to do. Equally, if you are not achieving what you say you want, then it may be that at some level you are resisting growth and the changes it brings with it. That resistance, though not conscious, is nevertheless there and deserves exploration as it is likely based on some past disappointment or hurt that you are trying to protect yourself from. As I have suggested earlier, it can be helpful (though by no means easy) to ask of yourself "How does this serve my purpose?" in order to bring into focus what it is that you are, at some level, trying to preserve or protect.

The vision for growth first finds its voice in the consciousness of the individual or group of individuals responsible for leadership in business. The very prospect of growth presents risks, not least because of the inevitable increase in headcount and costs associated with any professional services business. While the owners of a professional business may feel most acutely the potential risks of growth, they are equally often motivated to take those risks by the prospects of the success and reward that they present.

While growth may offer opportunities to others in the business for personal advancement and thereby greater reward financially and otherwise, changes that involve growth and development also place demands on those individuals. It will be natural to them to wonder and perhaps be anxious about whether they are individually capable of meeting those challenges and the associated demands placed upon them. As a leader, bringing others with you, sharing with them so that they may participate fully in the business of growth, is itself an immense challenge and one in which we simply cannot expect to please all the people all of the time.

Some in the organization may prefer that changes be presented as a *fait accompli* and that they be expected to simply knuckle down to the business of fulfilling the objectives that have been set. In this way, the individual is not asked to explore all the potential pitfalls and difficulties before they have occurred and is therefore spared the need to face any anxieties, justified or not. For this type of person, and I am making this overly simplistic, the important safety net and bridge to accepting change is that of trust. For them, the simple solution is to trust in leadership and to follow because that is how they prefer to operate. What such people demand in return for their loyalty is recognition for their efforts and an equal measure of loyal commitment from the leadership.

There are other people who wish to be consulted, who wish to have all information presented before them and to be allowed to take time to review, discuss, and question, much as though they were members of the leadership team. This group may never be fully satisfied with what is proposed and will accept that the decision has been taken and that they will, albeit reluctantly, continue to support the company and its objectives. There will always be gainsayers, those who feel it is their role to dismiss new ideas and any proposals for change, and to warn of dire consequences. But at the same time there will also be champions within the organization, those who are exhilarated by the opportunities and the prospect of growth and development.

It is important to allow these various groups to find their own level and not to seek to influence too closely how it is that the members of your organization settle into proposals for change. Consensus building in the context of a professional practice is always difficult to achieve; when it is apparently achieved, it can often be little more than skin deep. It is in the nature of professionals to consider themselves individuals, albeit individuals operating within a firm or team. No one, least of all a professional person, wishes to be associated with failure. The great challenge of leadership is to so encourage and reassure members of the firm of the growth that you wish to initiate that they are willing to put all their energy into their daily work and to share in the intention and the direction adopted for the business.

ENERGY

Energy is the essential life-giving component in any business and is derived from human participation, as opposed to physical or financial resources. Energy is the quality and source of creativity and application. It is the difference between success and mediocrity.

A firm with energy is one that attracts new business and keeps its existing clients happy and well served. An organization that creates an environment within which energy can flourish is one that has created a framework and platform for achievement through development and change.

Energy is at the most superficial level witnessed through activity and "busyness." At a deeper level, energy represents a capacity to learn and to apply learning in the course of working with others. Energy is the wellspring for readiness and attention. It is also the source of flexibility, adaptability, and cooperative working. It is a quality of emotional capacity and creativity that provides the conditions within which intellect and reason can flourish. Genuine energy, as opposed to the frenetic nervous kind that one sees in some organizations, flows freely in an environment that instils confidence and promotes a supportive and collaborative way of being.

Energy flows in commitment. Commitment is a condition in which an individual is able to say to herself that she is exactly where she is meant to be. Commitment is a state of mind and a state of being in which there is no desire to fight and no desire for flight. The committed member of your firm is one ready to put her energy at the disposal of the firm and to direct it to the best interests of the firm and its clients.

Without energy, or in situations where energy is restricted through fear, only the minimum is achieved and achievable. In a constricted environment, where energy does not flow freely, where control is the predominant factor at play in the firm's operations, little is done unless it is specifically requested or required. In a firm where the energy of individuals and collective energy of the members of the firm is not flowing freely, that firm is working well below capacity.

Human energy does not flourish in an environment that imposes formality and control. In this day and age, many professionals still think it appropriate to conduct themselves in ways that are no longer relevant to modern business or modern service expectations. The legal profession is one that is particularly traditional in its behaviour, often relying on formality and a misplaced gravitas to keep clients in their place and to discourage questions about the service provided.

Clients dealing with a firm from day to day and potential clients who might be considering retaining a firm will be intuitively and directly aware of the level of energy presented to them and effectively made available to them through their dealings with each and every person they come across in the firm. While some may be fooled, the majority will sense quite readily whether any apparent enthusiasm is actually substantiated by the type of energy I am describing here. When a client finds a firm in which such energy is available, that client is unlikely to turn elsewhere or to be attracted elsewhere.

In the field of legal professional service, the services delivered by one firm are essentially the same as those provided by other firms offering similar services. There may be very minor differences of style and format and these may, in limited cases, have some bearing on a client's choice. However, in most cases, clients are not making choices based on actual competence but instead basing their decisions on personal judgments as to the readiness of the firm to provide the services that they are offering.

Clients are quite naturally concerned with their service experience, and their perception of the quality of the service will be based upon that experience rather than any qualitative analysis of the specific work performed. A piece of work may be executed precisely in accordance with what was agreed and within budget, yet the client can still feel dissatisfied simply because the service experience was not a happy one. It is always the case that there is an emotional element to the client relationship; that element is one that is sensitive to and values the emotional contribution provided by the firm and its members. Energy is then very much a quality of humanity, a quality of human understanding and consideration, as opposed to pure physical and intellectual application.

Summary

- Commitment, readiness, attitude, intention, direction, and energy are all conditions that underpin performance and promote confidence

- Commitment arises when you are willing to believe you are, in the moment, in exactly the right situation for you and creates the mindset within which it is possible to find motivation and fulfilment

- Readiness is a form of alertness, being alive to all the opportunities that exist for you, and a state in which you place no immediate limitations on what you may achieve or how you may achieve it

- Attitude is about recognizing the opportunity, your potential to achieve and making the most of the time and circumstances offered to you

- Intention is the power we have to conceptualize and express desired outcomes, including how those outcomes will feel when we experience them

- Direction is the accumulation of commitment, readiness, attitude and intention so that you and others know where you are going

- Energy is the medium and driving force that turns intention into action and is often characterized as determination and enthusiasm

- Clients are attracted by and come to rely on service providers who are energetic in service of their interests

- Client service experience is determined by more than results and great service experience is grounded in great relationship

Behaviour

In this chapter I am going to recommend some simple behaviours that I have learned, put to use, and seen build trust and lasting professional relationships.

ACKNOWLEDGMENT

Acknowledgment is fundamentally important to each of us and no less important to those from whom we receive communication. Acknowledgment is the beginning of dialogue. It is the recognition that another person has made contact with you, sought to pass on information, or at least sought to gain your attention. Acknowledgment might be described as the opposite of being ignored, something that none of us enjoys particularly and which can be extremely disconcerting and irritating.

The method is a simple one. It is to recognize that a communication has been made and to acknowledge your receipt of it and what steps you will take to deal with it. When someone is speaking to you, it is important to give some indication that you are participating—that you have heard the other person, noticed that they wish to communicate with you, and are paying attention to what is they have to say. How many times have you encountered a situation in which you have tried to get the attention of someone, perhaps someone close to you, and found yourself ignored? It is, of course, the responsibility of the person initiating the communication to be satisfied that the other is alert and giving them attention. That said, however, when engaged in service we must anticipate that our clients and others will want to communicate with us and organize accordingly.

In professional service, clients and colleagues contact us by telephone, by e-mail, and increasingly by using messaging apps; many still also communicate by fax and letter. Each of these channels of communication are so common, so constant, and so familiar that we sometimes forget or fail to respect their essential purpose; namely, to communicate. If we receive a communication, our first responsibility is to acknowledge it unless there is a compelling reason for not doing so; for example, that you do not wish it to be known that you have received it, that you do not wish to engage in communication of any sort with the person initiating the communication, or that you wish to show disdain or disrespect.

In a service business, one never knows how important a communication may prove to be or how important the communicator may be to the future success of your career and, for that matter, the future success of your firm. Remember: every relationship matters, so act accordingly.

So what should you do when you receive a communication from someone? The steps are extremely simple. First, send a reply saying that you have received the communication. If you are able to provide a substantive response right away, then do so. If you are not, as is most often the case due to existing priorities, then the best course is to schedule a time (within perhaps the next 24 to 48 hours) when you will be able to provide a preliminary response setting out the steps necessary to fulfil the requirements of a substantive response and how long you think it will take to achieve that.

This very simple and practical courtesy was explained to me and to colleagues by Nicholas Gould, who went on to become senior partner of Lovells (now Hogan Lovells), when I was working there in 1983 as a trainee. He impressed on us the importance of responding promptly to instructions received from clients. He urged us to send a reply immediately, preferably on the same day (e-mail was not a medium of communication at that time), to say that we were grateful for the instructions and note when we hoped to provide a more detailed response. I have never forgotten that lesson and have done my utmost to be a good communicator. It doesn't matter that others don't do the same. The result is that I stand out as exceptional. I have had consistent feedback throughout my career to reinforce my conviction that prompt communication pays dividends.

Such a process has benefits on both sides. From your own point of view, it allows you to demonstrate that you have heard what a client, a colleague, or another has communicated to you and to give yourself the time necessary to reply to it properly. It also allows you to plan ahead to allocate time to provide that more detailed response. From the point of view of the other, it demonstrates that the message has been received. How many of us have left messages by telephone, whether by voice mail or with a person, and then wondered why it is that we have not heard back? For those who still write letters, it is expected that a longer period of time will be taken; however, similar anxiety can arise as to whether or not the letter has actually arrived at its destination.

When you do this, you manage expectations as well as your own time and responsibility—your "response-ability." Expectations and their proper management are at the foundation of a trusting relationship. The best way to build trust is to build it piece by piece, step by step, starting with the easy things. It is common for lawyers to become so preoccupied with the ultimate responsibility of providing the client with precisely the outcome required that the little things are obscured and forgotten. It is wrong, in my experience, to assume that a client who does not obtain the outcome desired at the outset will necessarily feel let down or badly served. Indeed, it can all too often be the case that the client has achieved the outcome required and yet has perceived poor service, becoming disinclined to hire the same firm again or simply open to using another provider. This is because the client expects the outcome that was achieved; she believes it could equally well have been achieved by another adviser. It is the service experience that keeps the client coming back for more.

One of the key aspects of new legal tech services is that users get what feels like instant response, albeit from a system as opposed to a human. These arrive in the form of a message confirming that they have been registered, a document generated by the system, an e-mail anticipating what their other needs might be, or an offer to call back to discuss service options. Web chat can be all that a user needs to help them to get what they want done or to take them to the next level of engagement with the service. The service given may be wafer thin in terms of legal service complexity, but the experience is a positive one and that's what counts. Traditional service firms do well to learn from these new entrants and adopt some of their practices.

Many clients suffer from a basic concern that their advisers are busy with other work and may not give sufficient time and attention to their matters. From a theoretical perspective, every client should receive precisely the same attention or at least the same quality of service and responsiveness. When any of us deal with adviser and other service providers, we quickly recognize when they are enthusiastic and active in providing service and when they are not. If they are not, what do we then do? We chase, we call, and we press our case so that we can bring our needs to the forefront of their attention. Whether it is an electrician or a plumber, doctor or lawyer, the story is the same: "the squeaky wheel gets the grease" is what we expect to be the order of things, and so we squeak for all we're worth.

A great deal of time and resources are taken up in dealing with clients who chase. Much better, then, to ensure the minimum application of resources by simply being clear with the client precisely when it is that you will be able to address what they have communicated to you. This practice applies equally to dealings with colleagues and with others outside the firm. Just as with all behaviours, it is far simpler, more consistent, and therefore more consistently applied if practiced in all areas and in relation to all interactions and relationships, as though every relationship mattered.

ATTENTION

Lawyers traditionally charge by reference to the time given to work on behalf of clients. Clock time is precisely fixed, universally known, and absolutely inelastic. Time recording systems faithfully record the number of six- or fifteen-minute units that will be used to formulate the accounts payable by clients. Clock time will pass whether we are using that time well or poorly. I want to deal here with the importance of the attention we give while time marches on.

The greatest gift, the greatest respect we can give to another, is our full attention. This is at once the easiest and the hardest thing to do. It is the nature of the human condition to be constantly engaged in thinking about ourselves. We are also greatly preoccupied with not just our private selves but also with our professional selves. Such preoccupations involve everything: details of office management, problems at home, small irritations such as delays on your journey to work or the fact that your favourite coffee mug has gone missing. There are so many things that can too easily invade the psychic space that we would better afford to others, listening to them and giving their interests our full attention.

This is not an easy challenge to overcome. I, for one, have needed and still need a great deal of practice in listening. We can all pretend to give our attention to another by fixing a furrowed brow, by writing furiously as another speaks, and yet how often are we truly giving attention to that which should be the focus of our attention?

This lesson regarding attention was first brought to me by Ian Jenkins, who went on to be senior partner at Barlow Lyde & Gilbert. I remarked to him that despite his busy practice, whenever I came to a scheduled meeting with him his desk was clear. He told me that he had been taught during his training as a lawyer that it is important to literally never put anything between you and your client or a colleague. Thus, he made sure that no files or other materials were in view that could suggest any distraction or interest in other than what he was discussing.

Another shining example that I once witnessed was on a subway train in central London. I saw two young people using sign language. Their communication was the most engaged and complete that I have ever seen. Their bodies were turned towards each other, their eyes fixed on each other with facial expressions and movements both conveying and reflecting what they were communicating. Theirs was a rapt attention and it occurred to me how poorly I communicate and receive communication by comparison. It is often said and generally accepted that something of the order of 7 percent of communication is verbal. How then are we to detect the other 93 percent of communication if we cannot give our full attention to what is being communicated and to the communicator? If our thoughts are elsewhere or focused on how something said affects us, then we are in danger of missing out on the 7 percent, as well.

These are some things you should never do: glance at or fiddle with documents or anything else you may have on your desk while someone is sitting across from you; type on your computer while speaking on the telephone (unless you explain to them that you are doing so for a purpose directly connected to your conversation); take a mobile phone call or telephone call in the course of your meeting (unless you have very good reason to believe that it is something so urgent as to relegate the importance of your immediate exchange with your client or colleague); look at the door, your mobile phone, or your watch repeatedly as though your attention were fixed on your opportunity to leave or something more interesting.

Every lawyer has many things to do in a day. There is a limit to the number of those things that we can think about at any one time. Thinking about what has got to be done involves little more than running through a quick list of what is outstanding . . . and then running through it again . . . and again. Going over and over what remains to be achieved in a day is of little value and contributes nothing to the achievement of those things. Thinking in this way simply jams up your psychic capacity. It is only possible for most of us to hold about seven ideas in our conscious mind at any one moment. In fact, when we are thinking about things, we are not thinking in the sense of generating new insight or ideas, we are simply rehearsing ideas or information that we already know, which we recycle like a cracked record. This kind of thinking is directly associated with stress, at whatever level that may occur. Stress physiologically interferes with cognitive function, making it impossible for us to have insight, to be creative, to innovate. It certainly makes it extremely difficult to listen.

Each of us knows what it is to receive attention. Indeed, it is something that most of us crave and find immensely rewarding, reassuring, and pleasurable. We also know when we are not getting attention and the feelings that can arouse in us. When we are not given attention, it can have an immediate impact on our sense of self-worth and our sense of the importance of our relationship with the person who is withholding or splitting their attention. If our encounter is merely a passing one, such as in a fast-food restaurant, then we expect little personal attention because of the nature of the transient relationship we are engaged in (yet how we respond to and remember even a moment's recognition, eye contact, or kindness!). By contrast, a relationship with someone who is important to us, whether personally or professionally, is one to which we are extremely sensitive and to which we give much greater significance.

We have so many tools today that make it possible for us to create efficiencies in the ways in which we perform our services. We can call anyone at almost any time, we can send messages that are received almost instantly, we can make complex calculations using sophisticated technologies, and carry out complex searches of documents in seconds; we can do so much so quickly that used to take so long. And yet we have less time than ever before. How can that be?

The amount of clock time available is the same and was always the same. In the days when it might take several days for correspondence to be exchanged, when we did not expect immediate responses, perhaps we did have more time. We may now be engaged in a less well-thought-out form of communication, playing telephone tag and sending one line e-mails and messages. These tools should be used to ensure that we have more time for reflection, consideration, and, above all, for attention to those with whom we wish to communicate. The expectation of instant response must be managed to ensure that people contacting us are reassured that we will get back to them—without interrupting what we are attending to.

The only time in which you can give your full attention to anything is now. The present moment, the moment in which you are engaged in communication with another, is the only moment in which attention can be truly given. It is too late to give attention to someone after they have left the room. The time we give may be measured by clock time, but it will always be valued by the level of attention we give in each moment. We have to make sure we attend. We have to show up. Completely.

We all struggle, to one degree or another, to bring "order in consciousness." We are constantly assailed by thoughts and preoccupations that distract us from the moment. Trying to stop thinking about something is practically impossible. If I tell you not to think about a big blue duck, see what happens. The answer to bringing order in consciousness is to first form a deliberate intention to give your attention to what is before you. Make it what you most value in that moment. Being present can be as simple as saying to yourself, "This is exactly where I am meant to be and what I am meant to be doing." In this way, you can place all of your available conscious processing power on what is in front of you now. You can get away with less, and most of us do most of the time, but it doesn't do us any good. It certainly does not do those with whom we are dealing any service.

Those who are able to give full attention to colleagues, clients, family, and friends—in fact, in any area of life—will achieve the greatest personal satisfaction and reward and develop the most sustainable and mutually beneficial relationships. Those who are willing and persevere in giving their attention are those who will be successful in the most profound sense; they are likely also to be successful in the economic sense.

Compare what I have said about attention with your own experiences with professionals, such as when you see your doctor. In general practice, many doctors have only a few minutes to spend with each patient if they are to keep all their appointments for the day. I have met with doctors who gave me full attention and also those who did not. One distinguishing feature of those occasions when I have received full attention is that I then felt confident raising some other issues that I otherwise would not have.

Consider the situation, then, where legal clients are confident that you are interested in them, in their business, and in achieving for them outcomes that they desire. They, too, are more likely to raise other concerns that are on their minds—and that they might otherwise not be willing to voice.

Remember, the well established 80:20 rule says that 80 percent of your work comes from 20 percent of your clients. In other words, the very best kind of business, and indeed most of our business, is repeat business from existing clients. In order to win repeat business from a client, it is essential to establish a relationship with the client such that the client prefers to deal with you as opposed to any other legal adviser. I know who I would choose to deal with every time: someone who I believe not only to be competent but also interested in me and my affairs. Someone who gives me their full attention. Who would you choose?

DO WHAT YOU SAY YOU'RE GOING TO DO

Consistently doing what you say you are going to do is the surest way of building trust in any relationship. Consider how airlines set arrival times that they know, barring exceptional delays, they can meet or better; one airline I have used sounds a fanfare and announces "another on time arrival," to the apparent delight of passengers. We like to know that our expectations are met and, if there is to be some delay, we like to be kept informed.

I was taught that as a legal professional my word is my bond and I must therefore take responsibility for the commitments I make. However, it is not sufficient to observe that standard only for obligations for which we could be held accountable and for which some sanction might be applied. Following through is a code and discipline that can and should be applied throughout all our dealings with others. To give our word is to make a promise and establish an expectation that we can fulfil.

One practice that I have used to great effect is that of pointing out when I have done something that I said I was going to do. Whenever possible, in a letter or e-mail or even a phone call or in person meeting, I use the words "as promised." I might say "as promised, I have attached the document you requested"; "as promised, I have spoken to so-and-so and established the following"; "as promised, I have made arrangements for our meeting next week." In other words, "as promised, I have done what I said I would do." Using these simple words reinforces and reminds the other that you are someone who keeps a promise. Consider how you feel towards a person you can say keeps a promise; then consider how you wish others to feel towards you and the benefits that feeling can bring to you in terms of the quality, openness, and ease of your relationship as much as in economic terms.

It is about the little things. After all, is not all of life, and certainly all of professional life, made up of an accumulation of little things? When you say that you are going to do something, for goodness' sake, do it; for your own sake, for the sake of your colleagues, or clients, or others to whom you have given your word and established an expectation. We must also exercise great caution in setting expectations, in saying what we will and will not do, and be sure to act accordingly or risk losing trust.

When you act in a way that is consistent with an expectation, then you are establishing confidence in others that when you say you will do something, you do it. That confidence can pay huge dividends when it comes to securing new work and referrals. Such confidence and recommendations are not necessarily grounded in a case-by-case evaluation of your skills, ability, and resources in a particular matter or area. More commonly, humans make decisions based upon their expectation of a certain type of behaviour or outcome; in other words, based on trust.

Everyone knows how frustrating it is when someone they need does not show up or follow through. If you say to someone, "I will get back to you tomorrow," then it is absolutely essential that you do just that. Even if you only contact them the next day to say that you are not able, for whatever reason, to deliver on their expectations until a later time, you will have significantly mitigated the negative impact of that failure by simply making contact. To make contact in this way is to demonstrate to the other that you are interested in their reality and what matters to them.

If you do not fulfil an expectation that you have created in another's mind, you are disturbing that other's reality, causing them stress and anxiety. The receiver of your promise, however small that promise may be, questions why the expectation has not been met and expends energy and resources trying to find out why things are not as expected. Not to fulfil expectations, particularly the small ones, is to say to others that the expectations you established are not important to you, however important they may be to them. This sends entirely the wrong message in the context of a professional relationship, where trust and confidence and assurance of service and dedication are what a client is entitled to enjoy.

Let me give you another example. In a meeting with someone with whom I hope to collaborate on particular project, I agree to produce a summary note of the conclusions of our meeting and draft some promotional material for developing our business together. The next day, I set about drafting the text. It takes me about two hours to produce something that I am happy with and I send the document by e-mail. More than a week passes without any acknowledgment. I call the person's administrative assistant to ask whether the e-mail was in fact received, just in case there was some problem with delivery. I'm told that the e-mail has arrived and has been read. Any guesses as to how I feel about that?

Another week then passes without any acknowledgment, response, or communication of any kind. Not a word. I am, of course, not aware of what other circumstances may have arisen that might have prevented the person from communicating. My thoughts are that this person does not value me or my contribution and, either consciously or unconsciously, this person does not regard our working collaboration as something worthy of attention. Is that the message this person wants to convey to me? Hopefully not, yet how am I to know?

If we wish to be in relationship with others to mutual benefit, then the process of relating to each other has to be undertaken with sincerity and with consistency. This applies as truly in our personal relationships as it does in our professional ones.

Doing what you say you will do is an easy win. It is the active display of empathy. Its importance cannot be over-emphasized. I urge you to be aware of it in every little thing you do. Do what you say you are going to do with all the little things, and all those little things will make a great mountain of things that can be the foundation of a trusting and lasting relationship.

EMPATHY

Empathy is now being written about as a strategic business skill. In her book *The Empathy Era*, Belinda Parmar writes: "Society is undergoing a deep-rooted paradigm shift toward a more human, humane and empathic approach to the way people interact." She refers to a variety of compelling research, such as:

- 96 percent of unhappy customers will not complain, but 91 percent of these will simply leave and never come back.
- 50 percent of every buying decision is driven by emotion.
- 90 percent of top performers score highly in emotional intelligence while only 20 percent of underperformers do.

Listening is a skill that is underdeveloped in most of us. The development of listening skills is central to any role in which a lawyer is likely to find himself in practice, whether that be management, mentoring, coaching, mediation, or any circumstances that involve interaction with another in the course of practice.

A great strength of legal training and practice is that as lawyers we learn to listen and record facts and information to which we can apply legal principles, legislation, regulations, and decided law. This skill is highly prized because it is a very particular form of listening that leads to a valued exercise of interpretation and application of the law. However, this form of listening can be so enhanced as to suppress another, equally important form of listening, one that addresses the emotional component of the client's circumstances.

Just as there is no human experience that is not first felt emotionally, in the same way there is no human circumstance that does not carry with it, within each individual and indeed each organization, a strand of emotional content. Emotion both enhances and distorts perception, and our objectivity as lawyers is held in great esteem because we are able to weigh up circumstances without that emotional "attachment."

When we are listening to a client, it is vitally important not to suppress or evade our first responsibility as a fellow human being—namely, to show compassion. Compassion enables an understanding of the emotional content of a situation as experienced by another in the context of any set of circumstances or any event. If we pity or over-empathize, then we risk being caught up in the same vortex of emotion that may have already debilitated the client and can lead us into a similar state of mind. This form of active compassion is also called empathy. It may be innate in some; it is, however, also a skill that can be learned and honed to great mutual benefit.

The emotional space is considered by most professionals to be dangerous territory; the same goes for personal relationships, where emotions can be challenging to deal with. When really listening to a client or colleague, it is important not only to listen to what is said and to identify what is perhaps not said, but also to understand and feel the experience of those circumstances from the perspective of the other.

If you want to learn how best to serve your client, then it is essential to understand what it is that your client believes serves him. To retreat from this opportunity is to retreat from the full and rewarding experience of close relationship. To exercise empathy is not to take responsibility for whatever stress or suffering may be experienced by the other, but simply to see it from their point of view and so to calibrate your response and communication in the true context and true language of that other's experience.

Some people take to this naturally, but most of us have to do it consciously and deliberately and check ourselves regularly to ensure that we are attentive to the needs of the other and to their experience. The very first step in achieving this is to remove our selves from the equation. If we place our selves between the other's experience and the service we believe we are asked to supply, then we will be missing the fundamental service opportunity.

It is important to recognize also that in listening we should not fall into the easy trap of categorizing or judging the other to be of a type. It is, of course, much simpler to categorize clients and colleagues as "easy," "difficult," "very difficult," or even "impossible." In most cases when people are being difficult it is simply because they believe that they are not being heard; or that their needs are not recognized or understood; or, in the case of a client, that they have chosen the wrong legal adviser. It may also be, just as in other relationships, that a client has had a bad experience with another legal adviser and that experience has coloured the way in which he deals with you. That is something you can complain about privately, although it will do little good. It is also something that you can take positive steps to address by building trust and delivering service that demonstrates your relationship will be different from previous ones.

Empathy is an active process, not a passive one. It involves an exchange between you and the other. There is mutual benefit in such listening. There is true dialogue.

One of the hurdles to true communication with clients and colleagues arises from perceptions with regard to hierarchy or to power in general. Many lawyers, if they are honest, would admit to a general sense of unease when it comes to dealing with clients. One colleague of mine was encouraged by someone early on in his career to treat every client as the enemy. This perhaps arises because we are constantly fearful of being found to be wrong to whatever degree or with whatever consequence, however slight. If the client does not get what she wants, she may complain to someone of higher authority within the firm, or perhaps to our governing body, or to other clients. We anticipate such complaints will be disproportionate, unbalanced, and unfair. Our behaviour can all too quickly bring about the thing we fear.

Clients, on the other hand, come to lawyers in order to benefit from their power (their power to deliver profit, protection, or on a principle). While clients may be paying the fees, there is element of surrender to the power of the lawyer to safely direct the course of a negotiation, litigation, or whatever the engagement has as its purpose. Very often a client will not admit to not understanding what a lawyer has told him. Clients will often raise questions after a meeting; they are not able to think of those issues during the meeting because their focus is on giving the lawyer what he wants (answering questions, making lists of things to provide, and so on) in order to allow the lawyer to perform his service.

One very practical way of demonstrating to a client or colleague that you have been listening to what they say is to repeat what they have said back to them or at least to summarize what they have said. In this way, the other has the opportunity to provide some correction or addition to what is essentially your report and interpretation of what you have heard.

In his book *Birth of the Chaordic Age*, author Dee Hock tells of his experience of meeting with a very senior member of a bank he worked for. At the conclusion of that meeting, and much to his surprise, the gentleman asked, "Young man, has this meeting served your purpose?" This was not a throwaway remark but rather a true question asked by someone genuinely concerned whether the other's needs had been met. Try asking this question in your own way when you next have a meeting with someone. Do so with humility and respect and you may be surprised by the result.

WHAT CAN I DO FOR YOU?

When you receive a call from a client or colleague it is seldom to check that all is well with you. It is generally because they want to ask you to do something or communicate with you with a view to you suggesting something that you might do for them.

It is a cultural norm for the other to ask you how you are and also perhaps whether you are busy. Though the question may be sincerely asked, it is not a good idea to enter into a long description of your medical condition or just how much you have on your plate today. If you say you are busy, then you simply discourage your client or colleague from believing you have the capacity or interest to help. The very best and earliest question that you can ask of anyone who calls you is "What can I do for you?"

One benefit of using these words—"What can I do for you?"—is that the question directs attention to what it is that the other requires. Should you even begin to think about how much work you have to do, or how you are truly feeling at that moment, you may well be so distracted as to be unable to pay attention or hear what the other has say. To ask the question "What can I do for you?" is the equivalent of leaning in during a conversation with another in order to demonstrate physically your intent to give full attention to what they have to say. This technique is well suited to the telephone and one that works for both sides of the relationship. First and foremost it indicates immediately that your interest is in knowing what it is that the other is interested in.

I always feel honoured and genuinely grateful that someone is interested to hear about what matters to me; being British, I already manage my enthusiasm for "sharing," and yet I still try not to abuse the kindness extended to me. Though it may make us all seem shallow, the fundamental truth is that what makes you interesting to others is your interest in them. I attended an interview with the senior partner of a London firm who, in response to my question as to how he enjoyed his role, spent almost the entirety of our meeting speaking about himself. He then reported to the recruiter that it had been the most enjoyable interview he had ever had.

If you do succumb to reporting just how busy you are, you will have missed an opportunity. If you are asked whether you are busy or whether you are well, rather than tell untruths, simply ask the question "What can I do for you?" to avoid having to answer. You will rarely find the other pressing for an answer.

Shift attention to the needs of the other and invite him to express those needs. It is only upon the expression of another's needs that you can begin to identify and then respond to any service opportunity. If you are busy thinking about yourself or talking about yourself, you do not allow space for the other to communicate their needs.

NOT KNOWING THE ANSWER

It is contrary to the instincts of any lawyer to be willing to admit that we do not know something. For some reason, most of us get it into our heads that because we have qualified as lawyers, we are somehow possessed of a responsibility to know the law—and not just some of it, but all of it. In an age of increasing specialization, it is perhaps easier to emphasize one's own skill set by saying, for example, "I'm a specialist in this area. You would be better speaking to someone else who is a specialist in the area in which you are interested." This is a way of avoiding saying that you do not know and suggesting that while you could, of course, deal with the matter, someone else may be better equipped to do so. As the years pass, we realize how little we truly know. Being at ease with uncertainty is said to be the measure of an entrepreneur perhaps because it is accompanied by an insatiable curiosity and appetite for learning. Nothing is assumed or taken for granted.

My suggestion is to adopt the Socratic approach—namely, "one thing that I know is that I know nothing." This may seem a little extreme, but

I recommend that you try it out. It lifts a tremendous weight from one's shoulders even if only said internally: "I don't know." The next part is, however, the most important when it comes to service. The second part of the statement is "but I will find out" or "but I will find someone else who does." This is service without the obligations of omniscience.

I will never forget an occasion when as a trainee I had researched a matter thoroughly and picked up the phone to a senior solicitor on the "other side" with the intention of engaging and besting him in a discussion of the law that would lead him to concede my view of the matter and a resolution in favour of my client. The gentleman taught me a number of valuable lessons in a few simple words when he said, "Mr. Rouse, I am afraid to say that I am completely unburdened by knowledge in this area and so cannot contribute to this discussion." One of the lessons was, of course, never to have an argument over the telephone. Sir, wherever you are, I salute you!

When anyone says, "I know the answer," I become immediately suspicious; doubly so when I hear myself say it. If I believe I know something, then it can only be on the basis of some past experience or information, which makes no allowance for any variance of circumstances or other change. It is, of course, reassuring to have order and predictability in aspects of one's personal or working life. It is also extremely dull. I strongly recommend the approach that allows for inquiry, reappraisal, re-evaluation, and learning something new.

There is plenty of room for creativity and innovation in the practice of the law. While the law may change slowly, perhaps the same ratio we saw in communication applies to the practice of law: namely, that approximately 7 percent of legal practice involves the law and 93 percent is about reevaluation, and service.

HONOURED GUEST

One standard of behaviour that I observed and encouraged others to observe when running my own firm was to treat any visitor to our office as an honoured guest.

The simple rule is this: if someone comes to visit you at your office, stop what you're doing as quickly as possible and go out to meet them. To do so is a very real sign of respect and always appreciated, particularly by clients but also by others.

There will be circumstances in which it is impossible to stop what you are doing immediately to show respect to your visitor without showing disrespect to another with whom you are engaged when the visitor arrives. However, 99 percent of the time this will not be the case and your first priority should be to greet your visitor. Think of it this way: if the visitor came to you at your home, would you leave him standing on the doorstep or waiting for you in the hallway? I doubt it. This principle should be applied whether or not your visitor has arrived at the expected time or has arrived without having made a prior appointment. The rule is the same: stop what you're doing and go out to greet them.

Just think how you have felt when you have been kept waiting to see someone five or ten minutes. We dare not complain; however, inside we usually do. Now think about how you have felt when the person you have gone to see, particularly someone of importance and in authority, has come out immediately to greet you. Speaking for myself, it feels great. I feel welcome, valued, and honoured. My sense of self-worth is not so precarious; nevertheless, every extra boost is welcome.

Adopting this kind of behaviour is essentially another way of giving, which is, after all, at the very heart of service. If you hold service close to your heart, then this is one more way in which you can demonstrate and express what is true for you. You will adopt such behaviour because it is what comes naturally and without expectation of a specific return, yet confident in the knowledge that "what goes around comes around."

PUNCTUALITY

This is one of those areas that can be regarded as old-fashioned. Somehow we have been persuaded that it is all right for us not to be punctual because so many other people are not, or because we are always cutting things so fine that we can so easily blame the traffic, the train system, or any other plausible excuse. A good friend of mine has expressed the view that the mobile phone has become a tool of delay and excuse for not planning properly to arrive at a meeting on time. Being late for an appointment says, "My time is more valuable to me than yours."

Making sure that you keep appointments at the times that have been agreed is not the hardest thing that you are asked to do. The only explanation for failing to be punctual is, in the final analysis, that you do not consider it important to do what you say you are going to do, and that you do not give importance to the impact your behaviour may have on others.

We are all used to waiting, but the nagging thought that comes to mind is "If you cannot be on time, then what will you do on time?"

In some cultures, it is expected that appointments will not take place at an agreed time. It is an English tradition to expect a guest to arrive approximately half an hour late for dinner, a blessing when you need the extra time for preparation. What is often called "rubber time," because it is so elastic when it comes to keeping appointments, is all well and good in a social context, but has no place in modern business and certainly not in professional service business.

It is very simply a deliberate recognition and respect for others to keep your appointments on time. It is also another one of those little things that builds trust, demonstrating that you are someone who does what she says she is going to do. Be impeccable with your word. Be on time.

Punctuality need not become an obsession. There will be many occasions when, despite your best efforts, you are unable to be on time for an appointment. This is to be expected, but it should not become the rule. If you are generally punctual, as I have always tried to be, then others recognize that and make allowance. As soon as you know you're going to be late, by even as little as five minutes, make a call so that others are not kept waiting.

Punctuality is one of those practices that falls under the category of good manners. At one time, good manners may have involved unnecessary ritualistic formalities and, thankfully, our modern culture has stripped away much of this. At the heart of good manners, however, has always been respect and consideration for others. Respect, consideration, and, indeed, kindness all still have relevance and importance to us. Punctuality is one of the ways in which we can and should demonstrate our regard for the needs of others.

Summary

- Observing a few simple practices can help to build trust and lasting professional relationships

- When someone communicates with you, providing acknowledgement to say that the communication has been received, and ideally a date by which you will provide a substantive response, serves to remove uncertainty and manage expectations

- Giving your complete attention to a client or colleague is the surest way of not missing anything important and making the person concerned feel valued

- If you say you are going to do something then it is vital that you do it, or explain why you have not done so, so that you deliver on the expectation that you have created and so build trust that you will continue to do so

- Empathy is most powerfully conveyed when you deal with others in such a way that, while you may not agree with what they say, they are sure you have heard and understood what they wanted to communicate

- When contacted by clients and colleagues it is safe to assume that they want something from you and the simple way to indicate that serving them is your priority is to ask 'what can I do for you?'

- Being willing to acknowledge to others that you don't know the answer to something is form of practical humility that not only provides you with the opportunity to investigate but also protects you from the pitfalls inherent in assumptions

- Greeting visitors to your place of work as soon as possible following their arrival should always be a priority and doing so is to treat them as honoured guests who have made the effort to visit you

- Punctuality is essential to demonstrate that you value the time that has been set aside to meet with you and though many will politely say that it does not matter, it does

12

Capacity Building

Capacity building is a term used frequently in areas such as international development, the environment, and community programs involving the human and infrastructural capabilities necessary to bring about sustainable development. Capacity building, of necessity, goes right to the heart of communities and institutions and aims to promote the conditions within which self-sustaining and self-renewing development can take place. Central to all of this is the importance of social systems and so-called social capital.

A law firm is a social system, a community of interest, and its social capital is represented by the reach and quality of the relationships that exist among those inside and outside the organization. The pre-eminence of financial capital has shifted over recent decades to intellectual capital, and it is now shifting again to social capital. A successful law firm that intends to remain successful will promote the conditions within which relationships can flourish. More so now than ever before, every relationship matters.

I have written here about the human condition and about relationships. These are of course inextricably intertwined, and it is not practical to attempt to address one without the other. I have suggested particular behaviours that can build trust, yet all demand sincere participation if they are not to undermine trust. We can all learn the words, go through the motions, learn to march in step, but that is just not enough anymore and neither you nor your firm should settle for that. It is time to take an active part in the inner game, taking individual responsibility through what I have called "self-management."

Managing lawyers is commonly compared to herding cats, a description that invariably raises a smile; yet this slightly bitter humour reveals much about the approach that has stubbornly held on in law firms. The idea behind this kind of thinking is that if they are not herded, these cats will simply flop about in languid disarray. This kind of management approach takes responsibility away rather than encouraging it. This approach fails to tap into the potential that lies within each of us to reach beyond our perceived limitations.

THE IMAGE MODEL

To make the best of our relationships with others and with ourselves, we need to do some capacity building of our own. I propose five elemental capacities that can be developed to contribute to success that is sustainable; all of these have been touched on in the course of this book. Happily, for those who have a fondness for acronyms, these capacities, expressed in their proper order, form the word *IMAGE*. These capacities work together and none is dispensable or less important than others. Trust in ourselves and in others is central and indispensable to each and every one of these capacities.

Intentionality

The power of our originating mind to envision and pursue what might be possible.

Intention is the stuff of imagination and vision, unfettered visualization, and free formation of ideas and aspirations. Though intentionality may eventually find its expression in language, its power lies in what language cannot fully express. However small, however incremental, imagining and making real what you can envisage is a creative act.

Intentions can be extremely specific as to form, time, and place, representing a precisely defined and measurable outcome. They can also be a desired state of being, such as a new office working well in a new

location. From the micro to the macro, we are free to imagine and define
to whatever   degree we wish, what we wish for.

There is an element of directionality with intention-forming. I think
of intention as an arrow pointing towards what we wish to create; the
sharp point and edges of the arrowhead cut through what separate us from
our goal. What comes behind is the full weight of the arrowhead, shaft,
and fletching that guides and prolongs flight.

Mutuality

*The recognition of our interdependence and the sincere pursuit of mutual interests in
every relationship.*

Our interdependence is the means by which we satisfy our most basic
need to belong while also being an inescapable consequence of our cultural
evolution. Acknowledging interdependence allows us to give to and receive
from each other in a mutual exchange. Pursuit of mutual interest is the
surest way to sustain any relationship.

The nature of our intention-forming is that it is self-serving pursuit
of what we desire or the way we believe things should be. Steve Jobs was
someone who, we are told, decided for us what we wanted as consumers of
mobile technology. Neither Apple nor any other business succeeds without
paying customers. In the language of the startup community, "social proof"
is essential if a service is to have any prospect of funding and growth.

It is all too easy to fall in love with your own ideas and to assume that
the world will want what you would like to create. Much as you may be
excited by your vision, you usually have to take others with you to make
it work.

Authenticity

*The natural authority in our words and actions when we are true to our purpose and
deliver what we promise.*

Find meaning and purpose and the rest will follow naturally. Being
authentic is our most natural state, although at times it is at odds with our
conditioning. What is authentic for each of us is something only we can
know and stay true to. Authenticity helps us choose what we devote our
energy to and in making that choice we invest what we do with meaning
and live "on purpose." We actively engage in the making of meaning when
we choose authenticity; each begets the other.

In an interview with Bill Moyers (broadcast as *The Power of Myth*)
in the final year of his life, Joseph Campbell, a leading authority on

mythologies and religions of the world, was asked to explain the meaning of the Grail. In answer, he said:

> The Grail represents that which is attained and realized by people who have lived their own lives; Nature intends the Grail. Spiritual life is the bouquet of natural life, not a supernatural thing imposed on it. And so the impulses of Nature are what give authenticity to life, not obeying orders from a supernatural authority. The Grail becomes symbolic of an authentic life lived in terms of its own volition, in terms of its own impulse system which carries it between the pairs of opposites of good and evil, light and dark. In Wolfram's version he begins with a poem that says that every act in life yields pairs of opposites in its results. The best we can do is to lean toward the light, intend the light; the light is the harmonious relationship that comes from compassion with suffering and understanding of the other person.

Doing what is authentic to you is the path of least resistance. I recall having to let go a young lawyer in my firm who really could not fulfil what was expected of him; he was a lovely guy, but that was not enough to allow him to stay on. Firing people is a hard thing to do, and I was not looking forward to my meeting with this person. When I told him, he became very emotional and tears began to flow—tears of joy, it turned out, as he thanked me for releasing him to do what he really wanted to do, which did not involve the law. He had qualified and worked as a lawyer to please his parents. I later saw him crossing the road while driving through London, and I called out to ask how he was. He told me he was having a ball selling photocopiers in between wind-surfing and skiing seasons. I saw a happy man giving everything to what he wanted to achieve.

Growth

The constant and conscious process of learning and integration through experience in pursuit of authenticity and excellence.

Growth can be a conscious process in which we challenge ourselves in such a way as to become more complex, building our sense of self and self-worth while at the same time gaining greater understanding of our interdependence with others and with our environment. Growth keeps us fresh, invoking our natural creativity and enthusiasm. Growth is the surest way to experience fulfilment.

A friend once told me how she had come to realize that comfort zones don't stay the same but become inexorably smaller, closing in on what you can allow yourself to experience until you find yourself closed off from all that might sustain you. Just as such contraction happens gradually, so too is growth best achieved incrementally and in such a way to engender confidence in your ability to learn and adapt to new and more complex experiences. You have to know yourself and just what stride length is right for you: enough to stretch you but not so much as to tear something.

I recall a poster advertising new apartments close to Canary Wharf in London's East End that proclaimed: "Travel broadens the mind; commuting doesn't." If your working life feels like one long commute, then find ways to stretch yourself to discover more of what you are capable of. Just the right amount of challenge stimulates us and brings the changes we need to be able to feel ourselves by pushing at the boundaries of our comfort zones.

Energy

That which we bring to our life and work through our cognitive, emotional, and physical powers and which we can release and direct in others.

Energy is our life force and its means of expression. Energy can flow or be constricted; it can be expansive and positive or restrictive and negative. Fear and self-protection lead to contraction; trust and confidence lead to expansion.

If you and others are not ultimately willing to put your personal resources, such as skills and time, into bringing about what has been envisioned, then something is wrong. It is our nature to pay lip service to new ideas and then not to back them with action when it comes down to it. New Year's resolutions are a classic case in point. The truth will come out, and whether energy is invested is the acid test.

Money is another form of energy, stored in a means of exchange. Money alone is never enough, but it can make the difference between success and failure. If you and others are not prepared to contribute or forgo money in order to support your intention, then you need to go back to the beginning and start again. It might be that only a small change to the original intention will be needed to be able to get back on track. Be sure, however, to go through each step of the IMAGE model again.

INTENTIONALITY AND MEMES

A strong intention can make "two oceans wide" be the size of a blanket, or "seven hundred years" the time it takes to walk to someone you love.

—*Rumi*

I would like to expand further on intentionality, which I consider the first among equals in terms of these capacities, by reference to memes.

Perhaps the single most important capacity we posses, and yet seldom engage consciously, is that of intentionality. The power of our originating mind goes wholly unrecognised in most of us and yet it is human intentionality that has created everything that is man-made.

While we have all heard of genes and have an idea of their importance to our makeup and our most basic behaviours; other factors, units of cultural information, are also of fundamental importance to our human experience as individual "units of consciousness": memes. The term *meme* was introduced by biologist Richard Dawkins in his book *The Selfish Gene* (1976) and has been defined as "any permanent pattern of matter or information produced by an act of human intentionality." Memes include everything from sausages to electricity, from football to quantum theory. What begin in us as ideas and imaginings take form in thoughts, expression, and, ultimately, in some physical or cultural form. We create memes.

Our capacity to direct our energies and actions originates in our minds and is represented by intentionality. This capacity is the seat of choice, the point at which we can intervene consciously to direct our will towards that which is good, authentic, and virtuous, or otherwise. Intentionality is the place from which we can meet Gandhi's challenge to be the change we wish to see in the world.

There is not a single method, technique, model, or process that will bring about authentic and enduring change if it is against our will. We very often tell ourselves that change is needed and can readily list changes in circumstances and changes that others need to make. Instead, if we work with our own will and originating mind, we consciously direct and form our intentionality.

A law firm is a meme; it is an example of an "imagined order" of which Yuval Noah Harari writes in *Sapiens*. A firm's name and notepaper are memes; its internal processes and traditions are memes. The culture of a firm is a meme and made up of memes constantly changing as a consequence of the incremental effects of the intentionality of each participant, albeit some exerting more powerful influences than others.

Some memes are fundamentally useful and so endure; others come and go as needs change and interests evolve. What is man-made is too often regarded as immutable and accepted as "the way things are." However, development and growth depend on our determination to innovate and thereby create new and improved memes. Courage is also needed in relation to some memes as they and their creators naturally resist any threat to their survival.

Just as present cultural memes came into being, so new memes can be created and become established. What seems immutable is only so because we accept it to be so. Legal practice and the workings of legal service organizations have not reached the limits of their evolutionary path. There can and will surely be change in traditional practices (in particular, in the area of ownership and reward models). There is so much scope and hope for those who wish to find authenticity and vocation in legal practice.

USING THE IMAGE MODEL

This model can be put to use in many ways: individually, in groups, or organization-wide. Each capacity can be discussed to find out what they mean for you and others and how they can be developed to mutual benefit (including mutuality itself, naturally). The relationship and interdependencies between each capacity can be explored and tested against how you and others experience the initiation, evaluation, and implementation of new ideas, however big or small they might be. Each capacity goes to the heart of who we are as individuals and how we want to work with others towards shared objectives and outcomes. What comes up may not be comfortable, and that may be a sign you are getting somewhere.

The IMAGE model is also a quick and useful test of new ideas. For example, the idea might be to develop a new seminar series that can be delivered at live events and delivered as an e-learning product for clients and as continuing professional development content for members of your firm.

Intention: Create and deliver new content that will please existing clients, attract new clients, and meet staff development and training needs.
Mutuality: Is this what clients really want and can't get more easily elsewhere?
Authenticity: Is this an area we really know well and can truly lead on? Do we have the skills to develop and deliver such a program?
Growth: Are we willing to put ourselves out there in front of clients and others, at presentations and "on screen"?
Energy: Are we willing to put in the time and money to make this happen?

If the answer to the last question is "No," then you have to start again at the beginning, perhaps reformulating the intention, and running through each step again; keep doing it until a commitment can be genuinely made to invest the resources, financial and otherwise, to make it happen.

Summary

- We can develop our capacities in many areas of professional life to bring about positive change and improve our relationships

- The IMAGE model comprises 5 capacities that hold value for self-management and for relationships with others: Intentionality; Mutuality; Authenticity; Growth; Energy

- *Intentionality* refers to the power we have to envision what might be possible, so creating new ways of being, seeing and doing

- *Mutuality* is concerned with the recognition of our interdependence and the sincere pursuit of mutual interests in every relationship

- *Authenticity* is about investing yourself wholeheartedly in the pursuit of what matters to you

- *Growth* is a process whereby we learn more about ourselves and others by taking on new challenges for which we must take ourselves beyond what we know

- *Energy* is the fundamental driver, and the power source into which we must be willing to tap, without which nothing changes

- Memes, regardless of magnitude or importance, are products of intentionality and come into being as a result of the investment of energy

- Memes are constantly being formed and it is open to us all to decide how we can create our own memes that contribute to innovation and change in our profession

Afterthoughts

I have set out in this book as many facets of professional practice as are practical given the constraints that I have imposed on my enthusiasm. My hope is that I have sparked your interest in aspects of your practice and your personal experience, perhaps even hit on some that are close to your heart. I also hope that there are other issues and questions that you feel I should have covered and that you will tell me so; this will mean that there is more for me to write about and more for you to read.

There are four areas that I would like to touch on briefly before closing: namely, mental health, success, partnership, and complexity.

MENTAL HEALTH

There is, thankfully, a growing willingness to acknowledge and address mental health issues in society in general and, though it is very early, in the legal profession. Mention of "mental health" is still generally taken as an anodyne reference to some serious illness or incapacity requiring medical attention: to say that a legal professional has "mental health issues" is to consign them to the "mad, bad, and dangerous to know" category of those who are not tough enough to make it in the profession. All the while, research shows that lawyers are more likely than other professionals to abuse drink, drugs, and their power over others; levels of self-deception and hubris in the legal profession remain high.

Why is it that lawyers require of themselves and others that they display no weakness? From my own experience, as soon as I responded to assurances from colleagues that I could confide in them and shared something of my troubles, that confidence was exploited. We expect our leaders to be strong and able to protect us from harm; they are the pack leaders and the minute they show themselves to be vulnerable, they will be challenged and, if possible, brought down. Clients buy into a lawyer's power to deliver what they want, and if a lawyer fails to deliver, then that can affect the perceived power of colleagues and the firm. Lawyers are expected to be "on it" at all times—an entirely unreasonable expectation for any human being. What lawyers learn to do is to manage the way in which they present themselves, and most will do their utmost to limit the circumstances in which they may be revealed to be less than perfect.

Mental health is perhaps best seen as a spectrum that all of us slide along at various moments and periods in our lives. We all feel low at times; we all suffer anxiety, loss, and other forms of unease at some times in our lives; many of us may also experience times of crisis in which our whole sense of ourselves and our place in the world is shattered, and from which we must recover and rebuild. I like to think of myself as having started life as a block of wood that has been gradually hollowed out by experience so that I have greater capacity to embrace what I experience and, like a Tibetan singing bowl, become more resonant. The more we understand and accept ourselves, the more we can have true compassion and active empathy for those we serve, particularly our clients.

Lawyers are under considerable pressure to perform and their work is invariably committed to writing or placed on record in some way. That this record may some day be scrutinized and held up to examination by a court or professional body is an ever-present threat. Lawyers work long and hard to earn their right to practice and it is arguably no bad thing that this should be a driver of standards. In my early career, I worked on professional negligence cases involving lawyers and accountants; all too often, the professionals involved failed to acknowledge their mistakes and made matters infinitely worse as a result. Mistakes are inevitable where humans are involved and the culture of fear that permeates so many law firms has its roots in the fear of shame and retribution that flow from them.

Errors and omissions are all the more likely when, out of necessity, lawyers have multiple concurrent matters to juggle; there is good reason for the common analogy of circus act that involves spinning plates on top of slender sticks that must be stirred constantly. As every matter also involves third parties, it is seldom possible to unilaterally control the pace or set the timetable. Kicking the can down the road is a common practice, which means that the real decisions are often postponed to the next meeting, deadline, or court hearing. Lawyers must work with a considerable amount of uncertainty with regard to so many variables, and when things don't go smoothly, this causes anxiety, apprehension, and stress. I am someone who enjoys the pressure of deadlines and competition so long as I can prepare properly so that I know I can cross the finishing line. There are times when we all have to "wing it," and that can be exciting, to a point. The accumulation of pressure has to have an outlet and, for lawyers, being overwhelmed is something that cannot be disclosed for fear that it shows weakness. The results are boorish and bullying behaviour, often coupled with the "Novocain for the soul" of choice.

If mental fitness were treated like physical fitness, with the aim that individuals train for competition according to their levels of ability, aptitude, and ambition, that would be an altogether healthier approach. Sleep research reveals how interrupted sleep has a negative impact on mood and cognitive performance. Working under the influence of drink and drugs, or their after-effects, can be as dangerous in professional life as drunk driving is to the safety of others. I remember being told after my first long flight as a young lawyer not to make any important decisions because, although I may feel no more than a little tired, jet lag would affect my judgment. This left an impression on me because it came from a senior lawyer known for his assiduous attention to detail, who was aware of how his abilities could be degraded by travel. Our minds are the product of the brain–body complex, and it is an inescapable fact that our bodies must be well rested and nourished if our minds are to function at their best. We should not, and our clients should not, accept or expect less.

The legal profession is replete with heroes who are working all hours and expecting themselves to perform like the characters of novels and movies who dodge bullets, fall off buildings, barely sleep, and yet vanquish all before them in the cut and thrust of cross-examination before a bewitched courtroom. Fantasy and self-delusion abound in law firms; everybody persists in pretending to be "doing great" when they really aren't. Elite athletes get specialist help with different aspects of their overall performance: a strength coach, a nutrition specialist, a physiotherapist, and help with the all-important psychology of competition. Lawyers are very much like athletes in many ways, but are in a constant state of competitive stress. Rather than medicating or using other unhealthy and unsustainable coping mechanisms, would it not be better for lawyers to recognize the demands placed on them and maintain a regime that supports what is expected of them?

Exhaustion and anxiety are like injuries that you try to work around by repressing or suppressing the pain in the hope that it will go away; by not dealing with the root causes, you only store up trouble for the future. Just because athletes have injuries and take time away from competition does not mean that they do not have talent, aptitude, and the drive to compete. Just because a lawyer suffers from a period of depression does not mean that his or her career is over. The billable hour has a lot to answer for, as does the collective greed of many partnerships that perpetuate a macho style of management that should have been left in the last century. It is these partners who believe that because they have a lot of money they have every right to impose the same tyranny they suffered under to "get where they are today." I believe the time has come to wake up to how humans really work and do something meaningful to ensure that we are at our best when we are in service of others. This starts and ends with self-management, and lawyers can take charge of their own lifestyles to ensure they perform to the best of their abilities.

SUCCESS

One essential message I have been trying to get across is that success in legal professional practice can and should spring from the positive and inclusive experience of every member of a firm. Everyone can and should take responsibility for discovering their own meaning and purpose in the context of their firm and their present roles within it.

There are countless definitions of success, including wonderfully shallow propositions such as "he who dies with the most toys wins." A more sobering proposition (borrowing from the title of John Gray's book) is that success is about "getting what you want and wanting what you have." Or you may prefer the words of Bessie Stanley:

> He has achieved success who has lived well, laughed often and loved much; who has gained the respect of intelligent men and the love of little children; who has filled his niche and accomplished his task; who has left the world better than he

found it, whether by an improved poppy, a perfect poem, or a rescued soul; who has never lacked appreciation of earth's beauty or failed to express it; who has always looked for the best in others and given the best he had; whose life was an inspiration; whose memory a benediction.

Because it is such an alluring proposition, success sells, filling bookstore shelves and auditoriums. We cannot buy success and yet we can certainly pay for it. We can achieve success and yet not feel successful. We can pursue the idea of success only to realize that it was someone else's idea all along and not our own. Success is a slippery customer—make no mistake.

Success is ultimately a personal experience and throughout our life and career our ideas of what success means for us change, just as we, ourselves, change and (hopefully) mature. This presents a challenge in the context of a law firm where individuals have come together to provide service while at the same time meeting personal objectives. It is nevertheless a challenge that can be met and in which there is tremendous potential for reward, variety, creativity, and being so much more than the sum of a firm's working parts. Success can and should also be sustainable.

Sustainability is a recurrent theme encountered across many areas of interest and expertise. The term is used extensively in the context of environmental responsibility where emphasis is placed on renewable resources: not destroying what cannot be replaced or inducing changes that may not be in our power to reverse. Much the same principle applies to success in professional practice in that achieving sustainable success for a professional firm requires that it be self-renewing; this can only be achieved through the constant renewal of the individual members of the firm through effective self-management leading to individual growth.

In a recent television show that involved Chief Scout Bear Grylls hiking in Alaska with President Obama, Bear asked what advice the president gave to his children. His response was that he urged them only to "be useful and be kind." President Obama has devoted himself to public service and made a great success of his career following these precepts; his is as good as any example to follow.

PARTNERSHIP

There is no question that partnership is special and carries with it a great deal more than a formal business arrangement. Though there may be hierarchy within a partnership, to be a partner is to be a member of a select and closed group united under one flag within one firm. Loyalty, collective responsibility, confidence, and trust are surely to be expected within a group whose members have chosen each other as partners. The opportunity exists for more than teamwork, more than cooperation, more than sharing profits.

A partnership is a community of practice and a community of interest. A partnership can be much more than the sum of its parts when partners are working together for the good of every member of the firm. The number of partners in a firm is commonly referred to as a measure of its growth and also as a measure of status or type. The sense is that a firm that makes or takes in new partners is made stronger. There is also the popular belief that a firm with more partners is somehow stronger; for example, that a firm with one hundred partners is stronger than a firm with ten partners. So much depends on what one thinks strength is in the context of partnership; a ten-partner firm may well be far stronger, in fact, than a hundred-partner firm. As the number in the partnership community grows, so the "partnership experience" can deteriorate; the opportunity is to reverse that condition.

It may be that there is a natural "tipping point" for the number of partners in a firm past which there is an inevitable decline in the quality of the partnership experience. This decline and deterioration is important not just because of its effect on the partners themselves but also because of the concomitant effects for other members of firm. If the partnership group is not a happy one, then the whole firm will suffer the consequences. If the partnership group is strong and confident in itself and its direction, then, in effect, permission is given to everyone else within the firm to work together in directing their energies for the greater good.

In his book Nonzero, Robert Wright writes about our cultural evolution as having been achieved through cooperation rather than merely through conquest and makes use of game theory to explain his hypothesis. Rather than being a case of "survival of the fittest" in which "I win, you lose" (zero sum), our cultural success and development is achieved through "win-win" (non zero sum). This makes sense in the context of partnership because, by working together, the partners in a firm each benefit and achieve so much more than they can alone.

However, it is also the case that there is a concurrent zero sum game going on that, in case it is of comfort, is entirely normal when seen from the perspective of millions of years of biological and cultural evolution. Wright points to an implicit bargaining process that is constantly going on, one in which we each monitor the contribution of others, whether consciously or unconsciously. He writes:

> In all cultures friendships have underlying tension. In all cultures workplaces feature gossip about who is a slouch and who is a team player. In all cultures people scan the landscape for the lazy and the ungrateful, and rein in their generosity accordingly. In all cultures, people try to get the best deal possible.

The tension Wright describes is, I suspect, fairly high in many firms. This tension is one that can so easily occupy time and energy and become a cause of disproportionate discontent. There can be repeated ripple effects inside a firm when, for one reason or other, someone puts their brakes on (just as on a highway when drivers brake suddenly and those behind are also forced to brake, eventually bringing traffic to a standstill).

While it may be perfectly "normal" that we should behave in this way, it is far from being a justification to continue doing so; its consequences are so detrimental. By being conscious of the zero sum game, it is possible to see things differently, to rise above it. Noticing that it is going on is the first step and the biggest step towards finding resolution.

Malcolm Gladwell's Blink and Martin Seligman's Authentic Happiness both refer to the work of John Gottman, a professor at the University of Washington and a marriage researcher. Professor Gottman is able to predict with extraordinary accuracy whether or not couples will stay together. A number of key indicators include what he calls the "four horsemen of the apocalypse": criticism (as opposed to complaint), defensiveness, displays of contempt, and stonewalling. When I read Gottman's findings, I was reminded of the sort of behaviour I have seen in action in the law firms I have worked in and heard so many complain of.

These behaviours are born out of fear and instances of slight (real and imagined), misunderstanding, and rejection that can create lasting distrust. The stress and pace of practice create the conditions in which relationships can be undermined all too easily. The inherent tension over contribution also provides fertile ground for growing dissent.

Buddhist teacher Thich Nhat Hanh talks about "knots" being tied inside us that can last for years and yet can be undone, if we are willing, through dialogue and forgiveness. The idea of a knot appeals to me from a visual perspective in that it depicts entanglement and constriction, and because it can be unravelled. These knots are mysteries when we cannot even remember how they came to be made in the first place, yet they can be untied. There need be no "lost causes," no relationships that can not return to their original confidence and vigour.

Professor Gottman is not only an expert in predicting marriage failure, he also predicts which will survive and thrive and has developed principles for making marriage work. Seligman has also created his own version grounded in key virtues and strengths and the recognition of those in others and in ourselves. Partner relationships have a great deal in common with marriage; there is much to be learned and applied from marriage research that can benefit partnerships greatly.

SIMPLICITY

A common subject among the authors whose work I have been studying is that of complexity. Complexity in the individual is synonymous with personal growth and the development of capacities that enrich the individual's experience. Complexity in organizations is associated with capacities for ingenuity, flexibility, and self-organization in interactions among people and resources. Complexity in evolution is the direction pointed to by what Robert Wright calls "the arrow of history," taking us towards greater integration and interdependence.

Yet complexity can be daunting. When complexity becomes too much to cope with, things get complicated. One example of this so often cited is that of "information overload." I will use the example of information to illustrate the broader point I wish to make.

First, a favourite quote, attributed to Oliver Wendell Holmes: "I would not give a fig for the simplicity this side of complexity, but I would give my life for the simplicity on the other side of complexity." If you think of knowledge as complexity, then information is the simplicity "on this side of complexity," and wisdom is "the simplicity on the other side of complexity." Wisdom is more than being able to see the wood for the trees; it is an ability to reach into the essence of knowledge with a perspective grounded in virtue and values. Attaining wisdom is a worthy aim for all of us.

There is no escaping the burgeoning pace of complexity in legal business and in the practice of the law. Everything is, as it should be, in a state of constant flux and the challenge is to do more than simply cope with it. The great problem with lawyers is that everyone is too busy to do anything about it, to get help, to find time to think again and think beyond. You can always wait to see what others are doing and then simply follow. Authenticity and vocation are, however, not experiences you can obtain secondhand.

What seems clear is that there is an opportunity to transcend our predispositions and influences of our genes and cultural evolution and that there is a pressing need to do so. One inescapable truth in my personal experience is that to get something, you have to give something up. However, in the field of consciousness, collective endeavour, and of the future, I do not think it is necessary to give up success, fulfilment, fun, or profit. What may have to be given up are some of the old ways, habits, and ideas of how we think things are or must be. Lawyers have a vital role to play in business, the environment, human rights, and many other areas of society and polity. New ways of providing service and new service opportunities are waiting to be discovered by those able to look beyond traditional and adversarial practice.

If things are to change for the better, then we must change for the better. We can begin by being willing to see things differently and to direct our intentionality towards achieving better performance and profitability through bettering ourselves and our capacities as human beings. We have barely begun to tap into the power of our consciousness or the power of human relationships. It's that simple.

Index